A modern approach to
PATCHWORK

A modern approach to
PATCHWORK

LINDA SCHÄPPER

VNR VAN NOSTRAND REINHOLD COMPANY
NEW YORK CINCINNATI TORONTO LONDON MELBOURNE

One has to know how to use tradition
without being strangled by it.

(Doris Schmidt, *Süddeutsche Zeitung*)

Copyright © Linda Schäpper 1984
Library of Congress Catalog Card Number 83-25963
ISBN 0-442-28039-4

Printed in Great Britain

Published by Van Nostrand Reinhold Company Inc.
135 West 50th Street
New York, New York 10020

Macmillan of Canada
Division of Gage Publishing Limited
164 Commander Boulevard
Agincourt, Ontario M1S 3C7, Canada

16 15 14 13 12 11 10 9 8 7 6 5 4 3 2 1

Library of Congress Cataloging in Publication Data
Schäpper, Linda.
  A modern approach to patchwork.

  Includes index.
  1. Patchwork. I. Title.
TT835.S3 1984   746.46   83-25963
ISBN 0-442-28039-4

Contents

Acknowledgements

I would like to thank Bob L. Bishop, who took time from a heavy work load at Parsons College in Paris to do my photographs, and to Joan Zinni Lask of the Patchwork Dog and the Calico Cat in London for the last seven years of encouragement in developing my own style and philosophy of quilting.

1
The history and origins of patchwork quilting

The first evidence of quilting can be seen on the statues of warriors in ancient Egypt, from about 4000 years BC. It is obvious from the relief and texture on the sleeves of their garments that a type of quilted undergarment was worn under the armour as a protection against the enemies' weapons.

The next historical evidence of quilting is in the early Middle Ages when the crusaders, returning to Europe after their long wars in the East, wore a quilted garment for protection against the cold.

Patchwork and appliqué were also in use about the time of the crusades. Each fighting army carried a banner showing who they were and where they came from. This was often a combination of patchwork and appliqué and was the forerunner of the modern flag. In America children learn about Betsy Ross who was commissioned to sew the first American flag using patchwork for the red and white stripes and appliqué for the stars. Most countries have colourful flags (figs 1 and 2). Today this tradition can also be seen in some European towns where a baker's shop, restaurant, or wine bar will have a hand-made appliquéd flag to proclaim its trade. A baker's shop, for example, may show wheat or a furnace; a wine shop may show grapes or glasses of wine in brightly coloured appliqué (fig. 3).

Quilting was popular in the Middle Ages at most European courts, as examples of

quilted waistcoats in fine, white satin and quilted undergarments and coats preserved today in costume collections show.

Later, when Europeans emigrated to America they took with them their knowledge of patchwork and quilting, introducing this skill for the first time to the new continent. In early colonial times there was no local textile industry and cloth and textiles came from Europe. The early set-

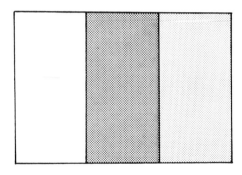

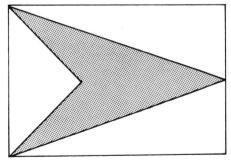

1 *Patchwork design used in flags*

7

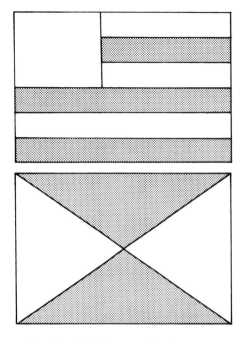

2 *Patchwork design used in flags*
3 *Appliqué used to depict shop motif*

tlers lived very sparse lives. Many lived far inland, roads were not yet developed and modes of transportation were primitive, so when shiploads of goods arrived from Europe it was difficult to distribute them to the far-flung settlements. What fabric they had was, in consequence, highly prized.

Quilting became a necessity as blankets were needed for the long winter, and when one wore out it was not thrown away but another stitched on top of it, thus preserving what there was left of the fabric. This layering and stitching together was the birth of patchwork quilting in America.

With time, patterns formed by the sewn-together patches and the quilting became more elaborate. Many from those times have survived, and are still being made today. They are still referred to by their old picturesque names, such as Log Cabin and Flying Geese, names that reflect the early American culture.

The early Americans were very religious people and believed that only God was perfect. A human being, especially a woman, couldn't make any perfect thing or it would be thought that she was trying to rival God. Therefore, in each quilt a housewife was obliged to make one mistake. For instance, if the whole quilt was made of small triangular patterns, perhaps she would leave in one square to disrupt the symmetry; if the design was made entirely of red and brown, perhaps she would leave in just one piece of blue. This same superstition is prevalent in India today, where Hindus making patchwork leave an intentional mistake in their work.

Patchwork provided the excuse for social gatherings amongst women in those early days when hard work and not much relaxation was the rule. After the children were all asleep a housewife would sew patches by candlelight throughout the long hard winter and then when spring came, and the roads were easier to navigate, all the women in the neighbourhood would come together at one home, bringing with them the patchwork tops which they had pieced together over the last winter and they

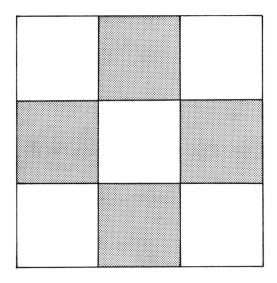

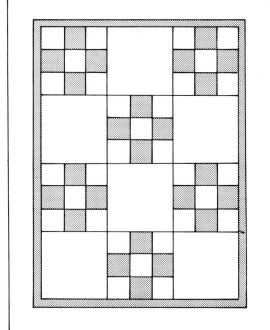

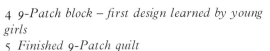

4 9-Patch block – first design learned by young girls

5 Finished 9-Patch quilt

would spread out the three layers over a large table-like frame. Each woman would take a corner, or part of the quilt, and the normally long and tedious task of quilting would be finished in a fraction of the time it would take one person. Their hands being busy, the women could gossip and talk to each other all day, even under the watchful eyes of their husbands. Very often the children stayed underneath the quilting frame and helped their mothers by pushing the needle through from the underside.

As young girls received no formal training, practically their whole education came from sewing. At about five years of age a girl would learn the alphabet and to count, as well as sayings from the Bible, by embroidering a sampler. At this age also she would start making patchwork. The first pattern would probably be a 9-patch figure (figs 4 and 5). This was a very simple pattern and helped train her for the precision that would be required later on for more difficult pieces. A young girl was expected to make thirteen quilts before she

was eligible to marry, and the thirteenth had to be beautiful and immaculate because the bridegroom was expected to look very closely at the needlework to see if his chosen bride would be a good mother and housewife. If she did sloppy needlework, it was thought, she would be negligent about other things. This quilt was traditionally used on the bridal bed and incorporated hearts, roses and other love symbols.

In India a similar custom still exists: a special appliqué quilt is made for the bridal pair which bears symbols of fertility to ensure that they will be blessed with many children.

The colonial Americans were a very superstitious people and did not believe in making the bridal quilt until one had actually found a bridegroom, and they never made baby quilts until the baby was on the way. Otherwise it was believed that these two events would never happen.

Wedding anniversaries, the departure of a favourite priest, or the birth of a baby merited a special gift called the friendship

9

quilt. Each friend would make one small section of the quilt, called a block, and shortly before the event, all the blocks were assembled and quilted at a quilting party. This practice also forms the basis of what is called a bridal shower, a tradition that still goes on in America today where the prospective bride is surprised by her female friends with a party and gifts shortly before the wedding.

The friendship quilt was reported to be very ugly, as each friend had a different design and colour sense, and the quilt was hurriedly thrown together at the last moment. It is said, however, that the receiver could barely see the gift through tears of joy. While a great many of the more beautiful quilts have lasted and have become part of museum collections, somehow there are very few friendship quilts in existence, which implies that once the tearful event was over the quilt was 'accidentally' lost or destroyed.

2

Patchwork throughout the world

Patchwork and quilting are usually done at home and, like other women's handicrafts – knitting, crochet, weaving and lace-making – are rarely regarded as a serious art form. In one form or another patchwork exists in nearly every country of the world and, although regional differences are quite pronounced, it is striking how many designs are universal.

Lebanon

Quilting is considered a profession in Lebanon, much like dry-cleaning, or tailoring. It is done by men who restuff mattresses with raw cotton in the spring. They then cover the mattresses with a bright gaudy pink or yellow satin. Since the satin is plain a pattern is designed on the surface with a simple but beautiful quilting stitch (fig. 6). The raw cotton inside must be beaten with a stick and spread evenly behind the quilted surface.

When I lived in Lebanon during the time of the civil war, I made 30 patchwork quilts. Piecing together the patchwork pieces is repetitious work, but its soothing effect helped me to cope with the turmoil going on around me. During the occasional lull in the shooting I would take my finished top across the city to the professional quilters. I worked with them for a year and, while we could only share five words of a

6 *Lebanese satin quilting*

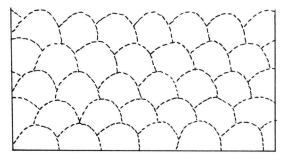

7 Lebanese pattern called Fish

common language, somehow we under-
stood each other well. One quilting pattern
they used, handed down through the gener-
ations, was called The Fish (fig. 7). I was
enchanted to see that it was exactly the
same as a pattern I knew called Scallops or
Sea Shells.

Once, when I was driving around in the
mountain area of Lebanon, I met an old
Armenian woman who was making the Log
Cabin pattern (fig. 8) out of the cut-up
remains of men's trousers. She had no idea
that this was one of America's most popular
traditional patterns. She had learned it by
watching her mother do it.

Ideas for modern designs can come from
many different sources such as my design
Robbing Peter to Pay Paul (fig. 9) which
came to me as I was looking at a cement grid
on one of the walls of a hotel in Lebanon.
The pattern for Autumn Leaves (fig. 10) I
got from a ceramic entry-stone to an old
house in a poor part of the city.

It is also possible to get ideas from
nature, such as the patterns on a tree trunk,
or a leaf (figs 11 and 12). Figure 13 is an

*8 Armenian-Lebanese
version of the Log
Cabin pattern*

12

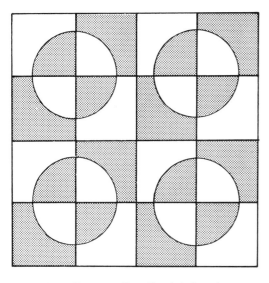

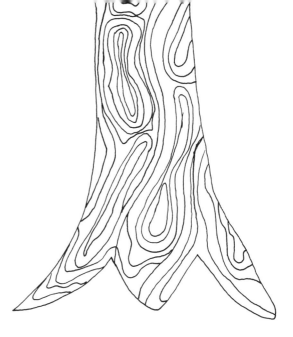

9 *Robbing Peter to Pay Paul (above)*
10 *Autumn Leaves (below)*

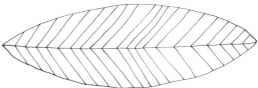

11 *Pattern on tree trunk (top)*
12 *Pattern on leaf*
13 *Lebanese appliqué (bottom)*

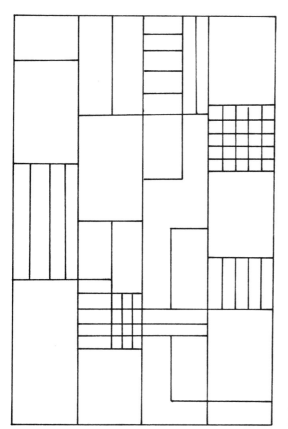

example of Lebanese patchwork done with appliqué, which is cut in one continuous piece without a break, hemmed under and then stitched onto a bright, yellow satin background. The seam is hidden by a twisted yellow and red cord attached all along the sewing line. The amount of intricate sewing in this patchwork is considerable and it seems a miracle that anyone would have the patience and skill to cut out the pattern and not make a break in it.

Syria

Figure 15 shows an example of Syrian appliqué work. It is similar to the Lebanese appliqué in the way it is finished. You can see the presence of a small twisted cord sewn along the edge of the appliqué, both to hide the stitching and to enhance the design. The colours are primary reds, blues and yellows. The finished piece would be used for a pillow or cushion cover.

14 *Syrian Bedouin patchwork*
15 *Syrian appliqué*

Russia

Patchwork quilting is as important in Russia as it is in America. Russian women have very little contact with the Western world and so have no idea that patchwork is done outside the Soviet Union.

Around the turn of the century, when the large aristocratic houses were still in existence, the owner of the house would give his discarded clothing to the most senior servant. She would take what she could use and pass the rest to the next important servant, and she would pass it on until the most humble would wind up with scraps, and the only thing she could do with the

16 *Russian patchwork found in National Museum, Moscow*

scraps would be to do patchwork.

Russian quilting technique is the same as that used in Lebanon, Turkey and Persia. The quilt is finished on the floor using a large running stitch and with raw cotton inside.

I was invited to tour the textile collections in the National Museum on Red Square, where I was shown among other exhibits the patchwork quilts in figures 16 and 17. Figure 18 shows the same pattern done in the American style, again an unexplained duplication of patterns.

15

17 *Russian patchwork found in National Museum, Moscow (above)*
18 *American interpretation of Russian patchwork (opposite)*
19 *Egyptian tent work or blind work (right)*

Egypt

Egyptian appliqué is called tent work (fig. 19). It is usually done in strong, simple colours of turquoise, black, red and white. It always follows the geometry of the Muslim religion. The name is because the large-scale nature of the embroidery is used on tents put up at religious festivals. It is an incredible experience to see the huge tents completely decorated with this handiwork. It is also called blind work, because the men who do it start as young boys and work until they are old men and blind. I found this difficult to understand until I visited the craftsmen and found them working in the dark, with poor lighting, and living on a very bad diet.

Brazil

Brazil is a very large country where many types of patchwork are done in the different areas. Patchwork is so common that people were surprised I would even be interested in talking about it.

One very popular type of patchwork is done in Recife (fig. 20). This is a truck-drivers' cushion. It is easily done. Small pre-cut strips of material are folded and hooked into a canvas backing, in much the same way as rug hooking. It fits the description of patchwork, taking small scraps of material to make an overall pattern, but is a novel way of using the idea.

Another interesting example comes from the capital, Brasilia. It is made following an old tradition, and is used here as a bathmat (fig. 21). It uses the traditional American pattern Log Cabin and is made entirely from the inside tape of men's trousers. Very often it is possible to read the name of the manufacturer.

My favourite example of Brazilian patchwork comes from the region of Belo Horizonte (fig. 22). It is done in the primary

20 *Truck drivers' cushion (above left)*
21 *Log Cabin, made in Brazil (above right)*
22 *Belo Horizonte, appliqué (left)*

colours of red, yellow and blue, on heavy cotton canvas. To cover the appliqué stitch, instead of sewing on a cord as is done in Syria or Lebanon, a crewel wool stitch is done all along the border, adding to the texture and the design. Patchwork of necessity should change and vary according to the availability of local materials and characteristics of the area. This piece of patchwork is a very good example and really gives the feeling of the tropical vegetation in the area.

Another interesting patchwork technique also comes from Belo Horizonte. Small rectangles of cotton material are folded (fig. 23a), folded again, and a third time (fig. 23b), and sewn on to a background piece of material on the dotted line (fig. 23c), leaving the upper part to fall free and give the impression almost of feathers sticking up, making a separate textural pattern. A similar technique was done in Russia at the turn of the century – it was mostly used for pot holders. Figure 24 shows a bathmat which was made using this technique. The pattern and colour arrangement shows a strong resemblance to an old American pattern which is traditionally called White House Steps, although I call it Homage to Vasarely because of its strong resemblance to the op art done by Victor Vasarely (fig. 25).

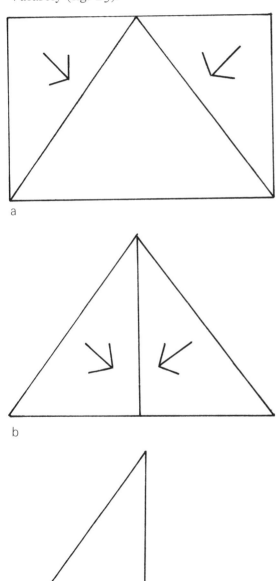

a

b

c

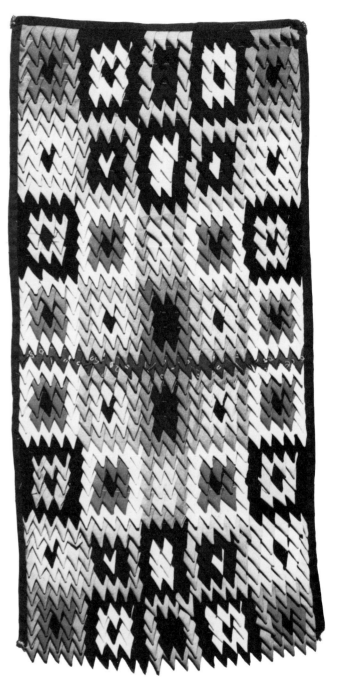

24 *Bathmat using folding process, Brazil*

23a, b and c *Processes in making Brazilian folded patchwork*

20

Colombia

Colombia has a type of appliqué work which could almost be considered mural art.

In this example (fig. 26) an everyday scene of village life is depicted. Embroidered stars twinkle against a dark sky background. There are trees and houses and a vegetable garden which is the central focus of the picture.

Panama

Panama has a very well-known type of appliqué called mola (figs 27 and 28). The actual technique is called reverse-appliqué and it is accomplished by placing six or seven layers of differently coloured material on top of one another. If you want green to show, you would cut through the first four layers until you reach the green and then turn it back. Maybe the red would

be lying three layers down, so you would cut through three layers and turn it back. It is painstaking work and beautifully and skilfully done. The subject-matter depicted on these quilts is often indigenous – bird, animal or plant-life.

28 *Mola work*

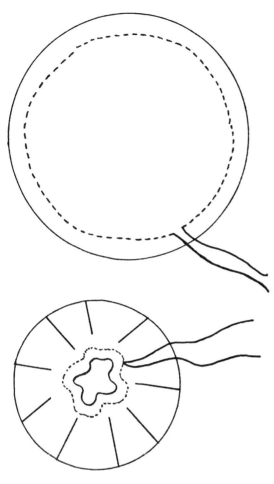

29a *How to make a Costa Rican puff quilt*
29b *The finished quilt*

Costa Rica

In Costa Rica I learned a technique already known to British quilters as the puff-quilt. Small rounds of material are cut out. With a running stitch you sew around the outside edge of the circle leaving the thread hanging on each end. Then you pull the threads, gathering the round into a small puff (fig. 29). The small rounds are then attached at four points on each, leaving a lace work-grid of connected pieces with space between. The quilt is attractive, although delicate. It is very easy for the threads connecting the small pieces to come apart and the puff itself may collapse.

31 *Hawaiian appliqué quilting*

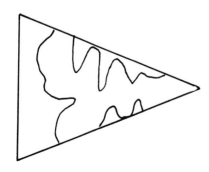

30 *How to make a snowflake*

24

32 *Appliqué animal from Kandy, Sri Lanka*

Hawaii

When the Christian missionaries went to Hawaii they wanted to teach patchwork quilting, but there was very little fabric available. They devised a new type of quilting which has become very popular in its own right. It only required one plain, coloured material which was folded, marked, and cut all at once rather as children make paper snowflakes, resulting in an identical pattern repeated throughout the quilt (fig. 30). The block often looks like a snowflake, but sometimes it is inspired by the tropical flora and vegetation of the area. The top piece of the quilt is hemmed, and then tacked into place with pins and then a basting stitch. It is then painstakingly appliquéd onto the background. After that is finished, the whole piece is quilted (fig. 31). The entire process can take about a year.

Sri Lanka

I have found two types of appliqué work commonly done in Sri Lanka.

Figure 32 shows one from Kandy, in the mountain area of Sri Lanka, which depicts an unrecognizable creature. As on all work from this area, the sewing is very well done and is decorated with a geometric border of small squares. The colours are limited to red, black and white.

Figure 33 shows a more unusual technique. This is a navy-blue pillow case with five circles of material appliquéd onto the background, and then the five circles are completely covered with imaginative embroidery stitches of several types which make an additional pattern on the appliqué pattern. The circles are then brought into the overall design of the pillow by connecting embroidery stitches on top of the navy-blue background. Although in some types of American quilting, such as the Crazy quilt (see fig. 34), an embroidery stitch is placed along the seam line to emphasize the pattern, and the blending of the colours, this is the only time I have ever seen embroidery used to form a completely independent, yet integrated, part of the pattern, and the effect is quite beautiful.

26

33 *Sri Lankan embroidered appliqué (opposite)*
34 *Crazy quilt with embroidery (above left)*
35 *Laotian reverse appliqué (above right)*

Thailand and Laos

Another very beautiful type of appliqué is done in Thailand and Laos. The appliqué technique is similar to the reverse-appliqué (mola), except that only one or two colours are used. The patterns are a series of geometric lines running parallel to each other. It also gives the appearance of a snowflake, and is often embellished with some well-thought-out embroidery stitches (fig. 35).

Pakistan

Nowhere is appliqué work more beautiful than in Pakistan (fig. 36). I have seen craftsmen squatting in small, dark, dirty huts, with hardly any electricity or natural light, the monsoon pouring down outside, small children coming and going and with goats being born in the corners of the room, but in spite of this they turn out the most beautiful appliqué in the world.

They also use appliqué as a decoration for their clothes, and figure 37 shows an example of the cutaway pattern for a decorative piece of clothing (fig. 37). The technique is the same as that used in the Hawaiian type of appliqué. The material is folded and cut out like a paper snowflake and then hemmed and sewn on to a background.

28

36 *Pakistani appliqué (opposite)*
37 *Pakistani appliqué (above)*
38 *Gujarat: Flying Geese (right)*

India

India has probably as rich a history as the United States in patchwork, appliqué and quilting, and all the variations of the three. In India each region has its very special type of textile art. It is an art that cuts across age, social and economic, as well as religious, barriers. I met a group of starving women working on a social welfare project in Ahmedebad who used the rags from textile mills, sewing them into brightly coloured patchwork similar in style to the patchwork done by the Bedouin in Syria (fig. 14).

Figure 38 shows a beautiful, strong triangular pattern done in the area of Ahmedabad. The red, burgundy and royal blue give it almost the impression of modern art, and it bears a striking resemblance to the American pattern called Flying Geese (fig. 39).

Patchwork is not restricted to the poor, however, as I discovered. One of the wealthiest women in India, the mother of the Maharisha of Jaipur, together with her ladies-in-waiting has made a hexagonal quilt out of gold and silver sari borders. In Lucknow the ladies of the harem use brightly coloured silk to make patchwork

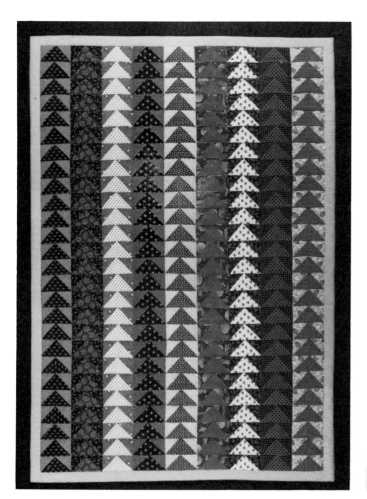

39 *Flying Geese (above left)*
40 *Lucknow silk patchwork (above right)*
41 *Maharashta quilting (left)*
42 *Maharashta appliqué (opposite)*

purses, quilts, and their bridal gowns (fig. 40).

The State of Maharashta is famous for making the very intricate type of quilting shown in figure 41. A plain colour is used in the central part and the quilting stitch is so fine and detailed that it looks almost as if it is part of the pattern of the material. This is a way to make use of old, worn-out silk saris.

Another example of Indian patchwork comes from this same area of western India (fig. 42). Each small piece is appliquéd onto a plain white background.

It is interesting to see once again how patterns are similar throughout the world. Figure 43 shows an example of quilting done in the State of Magda Pradesh which is very similar to the Hawaiian quilting shown in figure 31. The technique of cutting and sewing is the same; it often depicts plant life or local vegetation, and the design is usually achieved by using two colours.

Another example is the bold patchwork made up in the desert State of Gujarat using red, bright yellow, black and white (fig. 44), which is the same pattern known in the US as Bow Tie or Necktie (fig. 45).

In India, as in Syria, patchwork is made for several different purposes such as bed coverings and blankets, as a camel or elephant cover or as decoration to be hung over a window or door (fig. 46). Indian patchwork fully deserves study, and can give many ideas for further development of the craft.

43 *Magda Pradesh door hanging (left)*
44 *Gujarat patchwork (below)*
45 *Necktie quilt (above opposite)*
46 *Indian appliqué hanging (below opposite)*

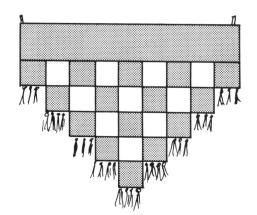

Afghanistan

The Afghans make patchwork in pieces and stitch it together at the corners much like the style from Costa Rica. It is used in the home and as coverings for animals. When I thought I had discovered three-dimensional patchwork (see chapter 6), I was much dismayed to find it had been done for centuries elsewhere.

47 *Afghanistani window decoration (left)*
48 *Beninese (Dahomey) appliqué (below)*

49a *Heading from a German magazine published in 1908 (left)*
49b & c *Patchwork patterns from the same magazine (opposite)*

Dahomey (French West Africa)

In the ancient French West African capital of Dahomey, recently renamed Benin, the art of appliqué has been used traditionally to depict the history of the African kings of Dahomey. Each of the twelve kings is symbolized by an animal or bird and other artefacts which characterize his reign. Figure 48 shows the history of the kings with their names and dates. The appliqué is enhanced by using bright colours and decorating it with embroidery stitches. In the National Museum of Abomey the entire history of the country is depicted in appliquéd panels, which look charming at first glance, but closer inspection reveals that much of its history consisted of cooking white people in little black pots and cutting off arms and legs with giant knives or swords. Nevertheless, the idea of depicting history with appliqué is an attractive one.

Germany

Patchwork is enjoying a revival at present in many countries of Europe, especially in Germany, where it was a traditional craft, as the patterns from an old handicraft magazine published in Leipzig in 1908 bear witness (figs 49a, b & c). The magazine describes several patterns which we still use in patchwork.

Switzerland

Switzerland has a tradition of quilting. Each home had a quilting frame up in the attic, very similar to the kind used for traditional American quilting, and young girls were expected to learn how to use it. Patchwork quilting never reached the height of popularity that embroidery and weaving did in Switzerland, but it was learned nevertheless.

Italy

Italy has a very special type of quilting called trapunto. Two layers of material are stitched together with a quilting stitch, and after one area is finished it is stuffed by threading the lining through the separations between the quilting. The layers are usually very heavily filled, and the entire pattern comes from the relief and texture of the overstuffed quilting. During the Second World War when textiles were hard to come by, many Italians survived through wrapping themselves in trapunto quilts.

Summary

Patchwork, appliqué and quilting are done singly or in combination, all over the world. The differences and the similarities are interesting in themselves but there are also many ideas that can be used and incorporated into our own approach to the craft.

3
Patchwork techniques

I learned patchwork by looking at pictures of finished quilts and just trying to sew them as best I could. It was what you call an education by trial and error. I made every single mistake possible, and as I learned better techniques I went back and repaired the pieces I made during the time of learning and experimentation. I have made over 300 quilts myself, sewing the patchwork by machine and hand-quilting them using the Arabic system of quilting which I learned in Lebanon.

Broadly speaking there are two types of design: geometric and non-geometric. They can be achieved by any combination of patchwork, appliqué and quilting.

I am often asked if one should start with a design idea and then look for the material, or start with the material and look for the design, or just start with a colour combination. The answer is any or all of these. There is no right or wrong way of doing things.

Beginning with the design

Colour plate 1 shows the design which is traditionally called Dresden Plate. The design gave me the idea of placing the colours as they appear in the colour spectrum which made all of them stronger, yet more pleasing to the eye.

Figure 50 shows a very pleasant simple

50 *Little Star*

37

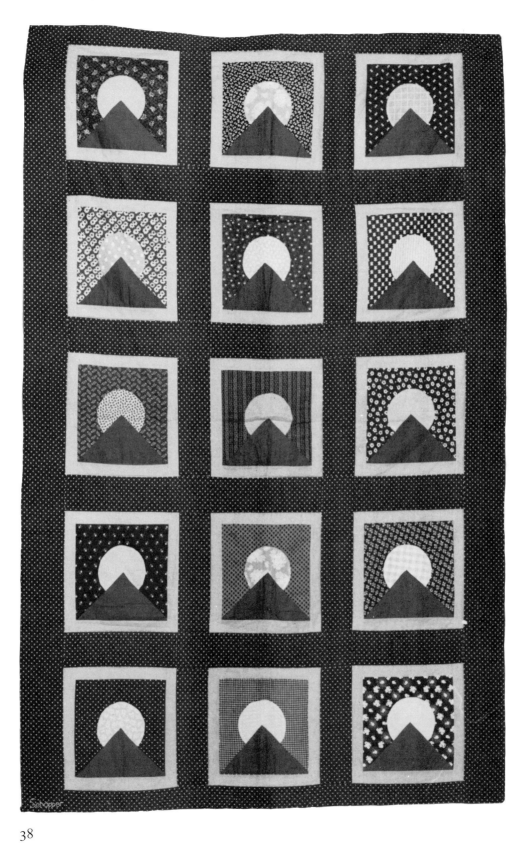

38

little design resembling a small star. I wanted to make something very calming, yet warm, and settled on a cream-coloured background with red-printed materials for the stars.

Colour plate 2 is a pattern traditionally called Mexican Rose, which I call Arabia because it reminds me of the type of design and colour one finds in the Arabian world. It must be done with three colours that are compatible because they lie so close together. This is a case of choosing the design and then looking for material to suit it. Red, black and beige are present in both the red and the beige background materials, and the black printed material complements it with the presence of small white flowers.

Beginning with a specific material

When I lived in Beirut there was not always a large choice of material available, but there was usually a blue polka-dotted material and a bright yellow one. When I wished to use up the spare pieces of material I came upon this traditional pattern called Moon Over the Mountain (fig. 51). It is made only with those two colours of material, yet the effect is stunning, a cross between modern and traditional designs.

Figure 52, Positive–Negative, shows another example of a quilt where the material came first and the design followed. I had two materials with the same pattern, one dark on light, and the other light on dark, and I thought it might be ideally suited for a design which made use of reverse patterns.

The traditional Irish Chain design in colour plate 3 was done by finding the beautiful blue, flowered material, and then looking for a design which would absorb the rather strong blue without detracting from its simplicity.

51 *Moon Over the Mountain (opposite)*
52 *Positive-Negative (right)*

Beginning with a colour combination

Footpaths (colour plate 4) is a design where I thought of a colour combination, brown and beige, and looked for a pattern to utilize it.

Reflections (fig. 53) is a modern design in burnt orange, navy blue and light blue. I had the colours in my mind for several weeks thinking it was a very original idea, and developed the design to go with it. One day I noticed that I was wearing blue jeans, a navy shirt and a burnt orange sweater. I had the colours in my subconscious and just adapted them to the quilt medium.

Figure 54 shows the design called Baby Blocks which is done here in pink, light grey and dark grey. Once again I thought I

had quite an original combination of colours, and then one night, as I was coming back from working in my factory in Sri Lanka, I saw that the sunset over the Indian Ocean was pink, mixed with light grey, and that the ocean had become a very dark grey in the fading light.

How to begin working

The most difficult thing about beginning patchwork is exactly that: beginning patchwork. When one looks at a finished piece of some 1500 small triangles it is easy to become frightened by what seems like an endless task, but like any process in life, whether it be raising children or getting a university degree, you should never look at the whole process at once, but rather plan

well, and take it step by step. It is a good idea to make a work plan for each day, either to finish a certain number of blocks, or a certain work process, whether it be ironing the seams or attaching a certain piece, and try to stick to the plan. Once you have worked several days on a planned schedule, little by little the whole piece does come together.

Today there is so much emphasis on creativity and individuality that it may seem strange advice if I tell you that a very good way to start patchwork is to copy another design, but I do feel that this is the

53 *Reflections (below left)*
54 *Baby Block (below right)*
55 *Star of David (opposite)*

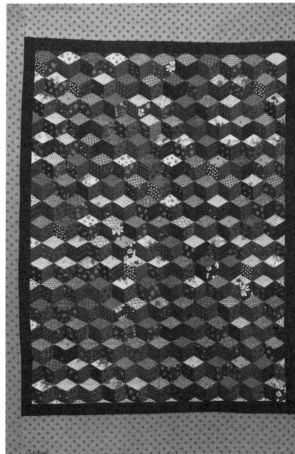

best way to begin. Very few of us have enough self-confidence in our own taste to be able to sit down the first time and choose something we like and be convinced enough about it to finish it. So if we do something which we have already seen finished which we know works and is attractive, it is much easier to stick with that. The successful completion of one project will add to your self-confidence, and after that it is much easier to start changing small details, or even using your own original designs and colour schemes. The first patchwork I did was the Star of David (fig. 55). There were 77 stars, and each one took 15 minutes to hem and place on the backing, and 30 minutes to appliqué. I did one a day for 77 days, thinking a quilt must take forever, and therefore stretching it to take forever, when actually the amount of time spent was not so much if done all at once.

The second quilt I did was the Dresden Plate (colour plate 1), and the third was Moon Over the Mountain (fig. 51). It was only after I had done those three that I felt brave enough to make my own original design. The Tree (fig. 56) was very simple to do with only the application of a circle for the leaves, and a simple stem for the base. I chose green material to represent the tree, light brown for the stem and frames, and off-white for the background.

Getting ideas

You can get ideas anywhere. I am always looking at floor patterns, wooden doors, ceilings, mosaics, church windows, and carpets. Once, flying over farm fields in West Germany, I got the idea shown in figure 57. The way coloured carpet samples were displayed in a furniture store gave me another idea, shown in figure 58. The wooden sun screens in front of windows which are supposed to protect the Saudi Arabian women from being seen by passing men formed the basis for Mouchrabieh (fig. 59). Flowers, trees or nature (figs 60 and 61)

can also be a source of ideas (see figs 51 and 56).

Planning the design

There are two different systems of working with patchwork. If you are making a modern design such as that shown in figure 62, the easiest way is to make a drawing of the finished design to scale. In other words, if the finished quilt is to be 1 m 50 cm wide, and 2 m long, then the small drawing should be $\frac{1}{10}$ of that, or 15 × 20 cm. Then, when you actually want to start sewing the pattern it will only be necessary to multiply the measure of the pattern desired by 10, and you have the cutting size. You do have to remember of course to add on $\frac{3}{4}$ cm for the seam on each side.

56 *The Tree*

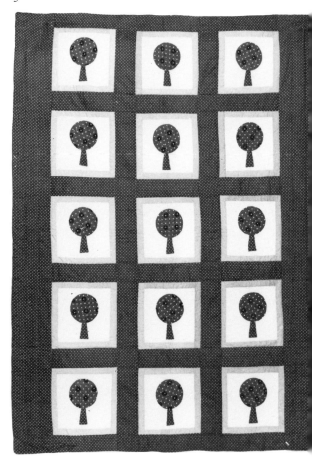

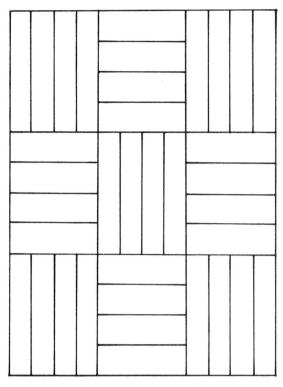

57 *Farm Fields over Germany*

The other way of working is called the block system. Instead of working from an overall plan the quilt can be made block by block. The pattern is made from the repetition of many small blocks, which, when taken together, make up the overall pattern. I highly recommend starting to work in this manner, especially for traditional designs. It is physically easier to work on small pieces, and it is also psychologically easier to set small targets every day. As I have already mentioned the most difficult obstacle to making the quilt is getting bogged down in the rather long and tedious work process. If you make a quilt with, for instance, 77 blocks, it is easy to set a target

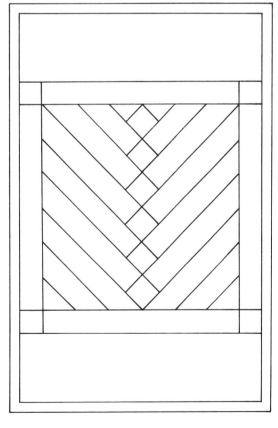

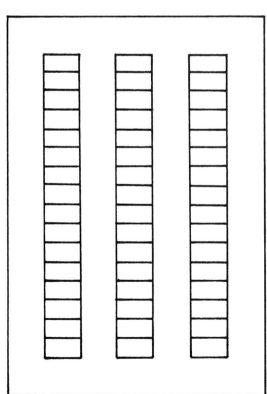

58 *Carpet samples hanging in a shop (left)*
59 *Mouchrabieh (above)*

43

of one or two blocks a day and get that done. To see the stack of finished blocks mounting up acts as inspiration to continue working and finish the quilt.

One word of advice. Mistakes happen! Even after years of making quilts, I still make mistakes in both designs and colours. Each design has some hidden trick which is not always possible to predict beforehand. Sometimes the mistakes can even be turned to your advantage. Waves (fig. 63) shows an example of this. In order to make up the zig-zag pattern the chevrons with a pattern on the front must be cut half towards the left, and half towards the right. If they were all cut in the same direction the pattern would merely continue in one direction. I cut them all going the same way, and then noticed I had run out of material and could not make the necessary corrections. Having already done so much planning and work, I decided to go ahead and finish the quilt, using the wrong side of the pieces I had cut out. The wrong side was a little darker than the right side, but, as it turned out, the slight colour variation added to the depth of the design.

I do recommend one thing, however; always correct a technical mistake. Even though you have kept all the basic rules of cutting accurately, sewing a uniform seam and sewing evenly, there are some mistakes that can slip through. Perhaps in spite of your carefully pinning the seams, they are not evenly matched. Perhaps you have accidently reversed the colours, or there is a little fold where one patch was too big and the other too small. You may not have the patience to correct the mistake the same day you find it. One does get tired and frustrated at times! Instead of finishing the piece and being stuck for life with an imperfection that could have been corrected, or taking giant scissors and slashing the whole thing with pent-up hostility, put it quietly away for a few days until you are fresh and can face it again. It will be like seeing an old friend.

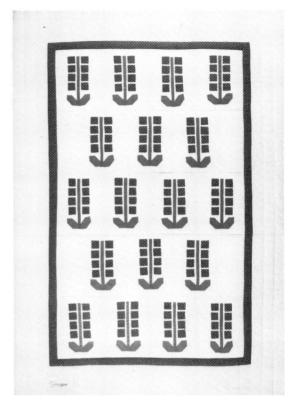

Working with colour

Another difficult thing to decide on is whether the colours you have chosen will be compatible with your environment. At first glance you may like burgundy, orange and olive green, but will it match your surroundings in the long run? I recommend leaving the material casually around the house for a few days to get used to the colours. If you still like them after seeing them in the morning when you wake up, at lunch and at teatime, then chances are you have chosen well. Sometimes you can also

60 *Bluebells (opposite left)*
61 *English Rose (above)*
62 *Blue Motion (left)*

45

63 *Waves*

64 *Footpaths*

be pleasantly surprised. I cut out Footpaths (fig. 64) in beige, brown and burn orange, and thought it would be very dull looking. When I finally sewed it together it was magical to see how the colours gave each other life.

People's colour taste and colour sense is as individual as their fingerprints. There have been numerous experiments to prove this. The same red was shown to several different people, and when they were shown that red in combination with other shades of red afterwards, each thought he had seen a different shade of red. Don't be afraid to do what you like. Some will agree, some won't. You are the important one.

Drafting the design

After you have decided what design you want to make and the colour scheme, the next thing is to decide the size. You can make a block very large and, because of the bigger size of the pieces you are working with, and the mere fact that you need fewer blocks, it is much easier to work with. But you can make the same design very small, when it becomes more time-consuming to work with because of the smaller pieces, and because you need more to complete the pattern (see fig. 65). After you get used to the techniques of quilting, you will probably find that a convenient, yet attractive, block size is about 20–30 cm but for your very

46

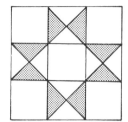

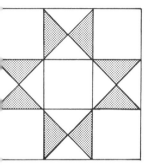

65 *Different sizes for the same pattern*

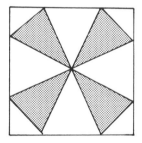

66a & b *Kaleidoscope*

first quilts I recommend using a block as large as 45–50 cm. If you are doing the design shown in figure 71, for instance, you could decide that the block should be 45 cms, in which case each section should be one-third of that, or 15 cm. If you opt for a smaller size of say 15 cm, then each block size would be about 5 cm.

Types of patchwork blocks

There are two different types of patchwork block. One is static. The block stands by itself and does not contribute to a second overall design. This type is easy to work with and the design is afterwards rather calm, and even feminine (see Dresden Plate, colour plate 1 and Star of David, fig. 55). The other type is based on a diagonal, and besides being a block on its own, it also contributes to an overall pattern (see figs 66 and 67). Log Cabin is a pattern which changes greatly depending on how the blocks are arranged (see figs 68–70).

Although impressive to look at diagonal patterns can be very dangerous. I once designed a block which I liked very much as an individual block and I had sewed the whole quilt together before I really looked at it. I tacked the piece against the wall to get a better look and saw for the first time the violent pattern I had created (fig. 71). I advise you, therefore, not only to sketch the block you will be making, but also to place it besides some similar blocks to make sure that the overall effect of a secondary pattern is developing the way you wish it to.

67a & b *Porto (below and right)*

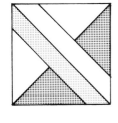

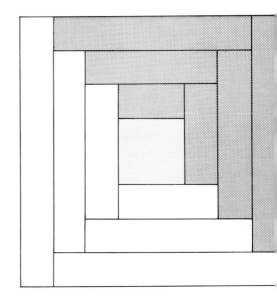

68 *Log Cabin block (right)*
69 *Log Cabin diamond (opposite)*

48

49

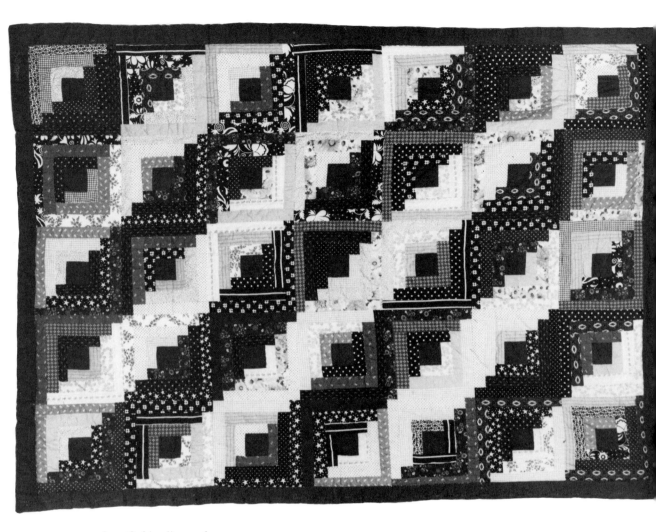

70 *Log Cabin diagonal*

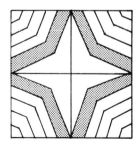

71 *Blocks changing when set together*

Piecing the blocks together

Besides keeping in mind the size of the blocks, and the way they will be pieced together, you can make some choices about how to set the blocks together. They can be set side by side right next to each other (fig. 72), or they can be interspaced with a plain block of material, either plain-coloured or patterned, to co-ordinate with the overall design (fig. 73). The blocks could be set with a small border in between the strips of pattern (fig. 74), or between all the blocks (fig. 75). This sometimes helps to calm down a pattern which might be either too strong or too nervous. It also helps to frame and accentuate a pictorial type of quilt (fig. 56). Another possibility (fig. 76) is that the frames become more decorative, perhaps spliced with squares of complementary colour to contribute even more to the overall appearance of the design. These are just a few options.

73 *Patterned block interspaced with plain block*

74 *Blocks set with small border between rows*

72 *Blocks set side by side*

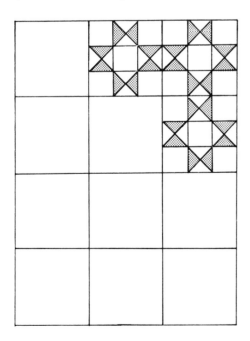

51

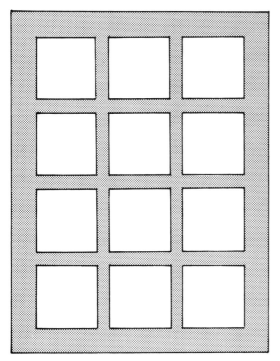

75 *Blocks set with small border strips between all blocks (left)*
76 *More decorative frames (above)*

Framing

The last thing that has to be decided about the design, before you begin calculations of the size you will want, concerns the quilt frame. You can design the patchwork to run to the edge of the quilt, or you can frame it, as I usually do, with a plain or printed fabric. I like to think of patchwork as a type of art and, as with a painting, I think the frame adds something. The frame can be as small as 40 or 50 cm, depending on the design, and how you want to finish it.

Calculating the size

Now that we have talked about all the different design variables, it is time to talk about the technical side of making the quilt. You have already decided whether you want to work with large or small blocks. Before you can do any further calculations you have to decide how large you want the end product to be.

If it is meant to hang on the wall you can make the patchwork any size you like. There are no rules. Measure the space you want to use, and work accordingly. Or just work until you get tired of the pattern, and then finish it off.

If you intend to use the quilt on a bed, then there are several different possibilities.

British system

In Britain it is quite usual for a quilt to cover just the surface of the mattress, as a duvet does. This is also an easy size to start out on because it is smaller, easier to handle and more quickly finished. To calculate this size, it is only necessary to measure the top surface of the bed.

American system

In America the common practice is to make the quilt large enough to cover the surface of the bed and to hang over the edge of the mattress on two sides if there is a board at the bottom of the bed, and all three if there is not. A pillow case called a sham, which covers the pillow during the day, is made with a large flange or ruffle and the quilt goes under the pillow to the top of the mattress. A skirt or valance usually hangs down from underneath the mattress to cover the legs of the bed to the floor. In order to calculate this you have to calculate the surface of the mattress plus the depth of the mattress on two or three sides depending on the design of your bed (see fig. 77).

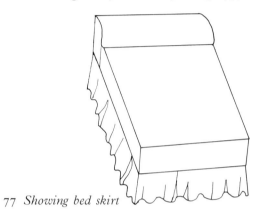

77 *Showing bed skirt*

European system

On the continent of Europe the common practice is to cover the entire mattress and let the quilt hang over to the floor. To get the correct size you must measure the surface of the mattress and then the distance to the floor on all sides. It is also the practice to fold the quilt over the pillows as if it were a bedspread, so you will also have to add 15–20 cm for that. On the whole I do not recommend this type, especially for your first quilts. A quilt should not be treated like a bedspread and be rumpled with daily use. The cotton and the delicate stitching suffer with the rough usage. It is also very difficult to work on such a large piece – although the patchwork is done piece-by-piece it is awkward to quilt the work when it is finished on the machine, or by hand, and really requires more than one pair of hands.

Calculation

If you decide that the size of the end product should be two metres, and that you would like to work with blocks of 20 cms, plus a narrow frame, calculate nine blocks across (fig. 78) and nine down, to make a total of 81 blocks plus a 10 cm frame. I usually try to work with uneven numbers as it gives a little bit more tension to the design than an even-numbered pattern.

Pattern drawing

The next step should be to take a very good ruler and transparent paper and draw the individual block exactly the size you would like to have it. In other words, if you want the block to be 20 cm, then the size of the drawing should be exactly 20 cm. It must be millimetre-perfect, as even a small error makes a difference if you are working with 1500 triangles. I cannot stress enough how important it is to get this step absolutely accurate.

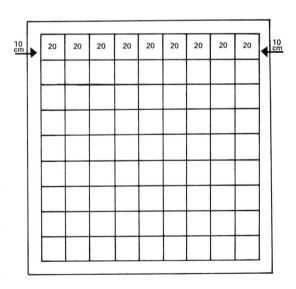

78 *How to measure blocks and put them together*

Making the cutting pattern

After you have made the actual-sized block pattern, the next step is to make the cutting pattern.

Figure 79 shows the blocks required for the pattern called 9-Patch. It is made of one cutting pattern, a square, and the pattern itself is formed by the contrast of colours, and usually achieved by using a dark and a light shade. Figure 80, Autumn Leaves, is made up of 16 triangles and 5 squares, usually using two colours, one dark and one light. Figure 81, Flying Geese, consists of a large triangle and a smaller one placed on each end. The pattern is made by repeating the three triangles in long rows. The Pinwheel is made up of one triangular cutting piece and the pattern made by alternating light and dark pieces (figs 82 and 83). Old Maid's Puzzle (fig. 84) is made up of a square and a triangle. Figure 85 is a variation on the Flying Geese pattern. I have renamed it Spring or Fall, depending on the colours. It is made up of a large triangle, of which there are 4 in every block, usually two of one colour and two of another, and 64 small triangles, usually 32 of one colour and 32 of another. The block for the Triangle Quilt (fig. 86) consists of two sizes of triangle, one large and one small. The part of the pattern which has the nine small triangles is usually made using dark and light shades.

Footpaths (fig. 87) is a very complex pattern, because of the use of light and dark to make the overall design. The actual cutting pieces are, however, simply a small square and a triangle. Study in Lights (fig. 88) is a simple pattern to make, but is made up of four different cutting pieces.

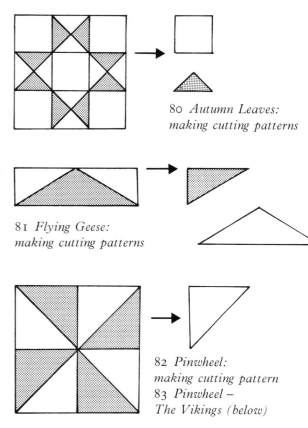

80 *Autumn Leaves: making cutting patterns*

81 *Flying Geese: making cutting patterns*

82 *Pinwheel: making cutting pattern*
83 *Pinwheel – The Vikings (below)*

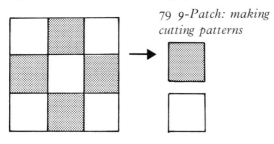

79 *9-Patch: making cutting patterns*

54

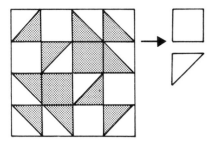

84 *Puzzle: making cutting patterns*

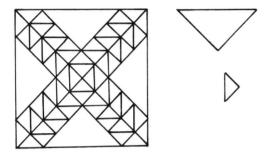

85 *Spring Pattern: making cutting patterns*

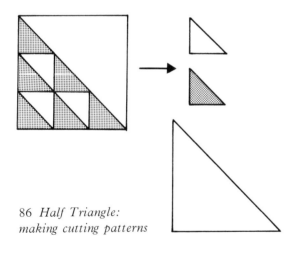

86 *Half Triangle:*
making cutting patterns

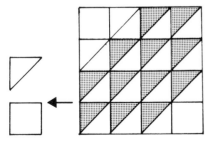

87 *Footpaths: making cutting patterns*

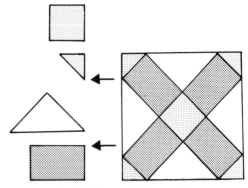

88 *Study in Lights: making cutting patterns*

Making the templates

When you have drawn the cutting pieces which will make up the pattern block, place the tracing paper over a piece of cardboard and, with a ruler and ballpoint pen, transfer the outline of each individual cutting piece onto the cardboard by pressing hard with the ballpoint pen into the cardboard. Then ink in the indentation. You must now add on a little for the seam allowance. I usually add $\frac{3}{4}$ cm on all sides, but you could add less or more, depending on what you feel comfortable with. Now cut out your pieces from the cardboard and you have your templates for cutting round.

Even though you have been accurate and careful throughout the drawing stages, it really is a good idea to make one test block. That way any inaccuracies will show up before you begin to make the whole quilt.

I also strongly recommend calculating how many triangles, squares, etc. you will need and in what colours before you even begin cutting. It is very tempting to start cutting out a few in one colour and a few in another but this is the wrong way to go about it. It is much faster in the long run to cut all the colours and shapes at the same time. At this particular stage stopping and starting is more time-consuming than doing the whole process at once. Also, you may run out of material and it is heartbreaking to work days or weeks on a project and then find you don't have enough ma-

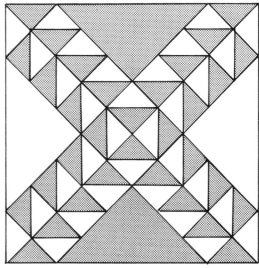

89 *Variation on Flying Geese (above)*
90 *Spring Pattern (right)*

terial to finish the last three squares. I made this mistake once when making a variation of the Flying Geese pattern (fig. 89). I cut and sewed the patchwork together without calculating enough for the frame, which I wanted to be of the same olive-green flowered material. By the time I discovered that I needed more olive material it was sold out.

How to calculate the total pieces needed

Let's take Spring (fig. 90) as an example. Let's say that each block is 45 cm square, and I want the end length to be 160 × 210 cm. Three times 45 cm would be 135 cm which is just about the right width, and 4 times 45 cm is 180 cm which is just about the right length. If I added a border of between 25 and 30 cm, I would achieve the desired size. Looking at figure 90 we can see that we need 2 large triangles of one colour, × 12, which equals 24, and 2 large triangles of another colour, × 12, which also equals 24. We also need 32 triangles of one colour × 12 which equals a total of 384, and also 32 triangles of another colour which equals 384 of a second colour. So before we begin we know the total amount needed.

Cutting out

Now that you have made the templates and have calculated the amount of pieces needed, the next step is to sit down and draw out the required amount. Figure 91 shows the way I usually draw, placing the cutting pattern along the bottom straight edge of the material, and marking row after row. This is fast, since the stroke of the scissors cuts out two triangles at once, and it is quite accurate. It is very important that the pattern is cut on a straight edge, and the long edge of the pattern should always be cut with the grain. If you cut some with and some against the grain, you could perhaps save on material, but the tension is not right when you come to sew the pieces together.

Test wash all materials

I recommend test washing all cotton before use. You can cut a piece ten centimetres square, wash it and leave it on a piece of newspaper to dry. If it bleeds, or shrinks then the whole piece must be washed. Cotton is unpredictable. A cheap cotton may turn out to be of good quality, whereas a very expensive one may both run and shrink.

Sewing techniques

I never give any advice on how the patchwork should be sewn together. I personally have always used a sewing machine because the stitch is straighter, firmer and less likely to fall apart or look crooked. There are some fanatics who believe that because traditionally patchwork was sewn by hand, it must also be sewn by hand today. But, after all, patchwork is a folk art, and it should reflect the age we are in. When there were no sewing machines, it was sewn by hand. Today we have the choice. For those who like to be able to say they did the whole quilt by hand and who wish to sew pieces together on the bus or in front of the TV, then hand-sewing is the answer. For those who prefer speed, machine-sewing is also acceptable. There is no right or wrong, only what you feel comfortable with.

91 *How to lay out triangles for cutting*

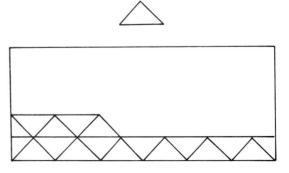

Beginning the sewing

You must first work out which parts of the puzzle go together. I usually do all the like steps at the same time, for instance for the Triangle quilt, the first step would be to sew the triangles along the longer side together to make a square (fig. 92). One day's work could then be to sew all the dark triangles and light triangles together. The second step is to start making rows, so the second day's work plan could be to complete all the row-work. Basically it is a matter of building up elements. After you have done three rows, half the block is complete, and the last step is to sew the two halves together. The Necktie is also easy. You attach two triangles along the short side, duplicate the same for the second pair of triangles, and then attach the square (fig. 93).

Even the most complex block is simple when you do it in this step-by-step process. In 9-Patch (fig. 94) you would first sew the rows together and then the block. Rhythm and Blues (figs 95 and 96), so-called because of the preponderance of blue, is a very modern design and is very easy to put together. I made the drawing to scale. Each strip measures 5 cm $\times$ 14 cm, therefore all you have to do is multiply that by 10, and add on the $\frac{3}{4}$ cm for the seam allowance. So, I cut narrow strips measuring $6\frac{1}{2}$ cm $\times$ $141\frac{1}{2}$ cm and sew them together.

Another very modern but easily accomplished design is Mouchrabieh (fig. 97). First, complete the middle section, dividing it into squares and triangles and then piece together blocks and then rows. The triangles make the corners at the ends of the rows. After the main patchwork is complete, proceed with the first border, measuring very carefullly. I made the pat-

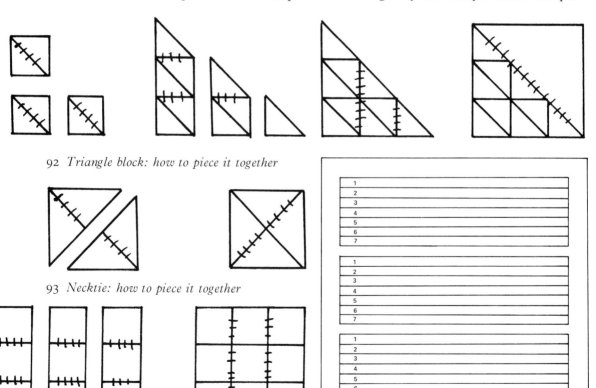

92 *Triangle block: how to piece it together*

93 *Necktie: how to piece it together*

94 *9-Patch: how to piece it together*

95 *Rhythm and Blues*

96 *Rhythm and Blues*
(above)
97 *Mouchrabieh (left)*

59

tern in turquoise, red and violet, and it turned out to be very strong. Afterwards I was asked to adapt the design to a beige office setting, and changed the colours to brown, beige and yellow, and the entire design became soft and warm.

Seams

I used to iron the seams open thinking that flatness was necessary, but when I started to make patchwork on a commercial basis it was no longer possible to iron open every seam, so I regretfully compromised and allowed the seams to be ironed to one side. Much to my surprise I discovered that it made hardly any difference at all to the finished appearance of the quilt.

Pinking or trimming the seams is not necessary because the seams become invisible within the three layers of material in the finished quilt. I usually trim the corners off the triangles, and very often when, in spite of my best intentions, the patchwork is not even, I adjust it with the scissors. As much as you try for perfection in patchwork, because of the flexibility of textiles, especially cotton, there is always a slight give and take and partial inaccuracy. Ironing and trimming should help this.

Sewing blocks together

When you have made the required number of blocks, the next step is to sew the blocks together. Do this in the same logical order that you made the block. First sew together one row, then another, and then when all the rows are made you can lay out the overall pattern either on a table or the carpet to check the overall effect. Only at that point can you attach all the rows to make the entire centrepiece. In order to get the seams completely straight I always pin each one making sure they are evenly matched. But once again, some people find it easier to sew the seam directly with a sewing machine.

Framing

No matter how we plan and measure there is always a slight difference in the length of the patchwork on one side compared to the other. If you sew a border of the same width all the way round the tendency is that the edges stretch and the border will at times be so big that it looks like a ruffle. It is best to measure the patchwork from top to bottom in at least three places along each side. If you had intended one side to be 180 cm, it is quite possible that the first measurement would be 176 cm, the second 184 cm and the third 182 cm. What I do is take the average, here about 180 cm, and pre-measure and pre-cut the border to this length. I then pin the border along the two opposite sides, making sure that they are evenly spaced, and only then do I sew them on. Once the top and bottom border are attached, I repeat the process for the two side borders.

Other types of border possibilities

You may find it more interesting to decorate the border with other designs, or even with the same pattern used for the patchwork. Figures 98 and 99 show some further ideas. Another method is leaving the edge scalloped, or with triangles overlapping; there are many possibilities.

Appliqué

There are a few things which should be mentioned about appliqué before we proceed to the quilting section.

Appliqué may be done by hand or by the machine. One way is to draw the pattern, whether it be a leaf or flower, with the sewing seam. After cutting, hem it with a running stitch, and then pin it onto the background. To make sure the pieces are attached symmetrically, you can fold the block in half and then in quarters, leaving the fold mark. You can use those lines as a gauge. Proceed to appliqué the pieces onto

the background, using a hemming stitch.

If you are doing appliqué on a machine, leave about a centimetre or more of seam around the piece to be appliquéd. Place it on the backing and, using the zig-zag stitch on the machine, carefully sew around the drawn line. When you have done that, cut away the excess material remaining after sewing with a small pair of scissors.

When you have finished the individual appliquéd blocks, you set them row by row and then make the inside piece and frame it as desired.

98 and 99 *Border possibilities*

Quilting

Regardless of the technique you have used, whether patchwork, traditional or modern, or appliqué, when you have finished the top piece, the next steps are the same.

For me, the last step, quilting, is the most fun and rewarding, because even the most primitive-looking patchwork looks better after it acquires the texture, weight, and decoration of the quilting process. Many beautiful patchwork pieces are hiding in closets all over the world because their makers didn't know how to go on.

There are several different methods of finishing up the quilt, and I would like to mention some of the advantages and disadvantages of each. I learned quilting by hand but I have also had extensive experience with machine-quilting and, quite honestly, there is not much difference in the overall effect of a beautiful patchwork quilt if it is finished by hand or machine.

The filling

Whether the quilting is done by hand or machine, you must choose a filling. In earlier times, women used leaves and tree bark, but most of these quilts did not last very long because of the abrasiveness of this filling material. Flannel sheets or worn-out blankets can also be used.

In the Middle East, where I learned to quilt, raw cotton is used. First it is run through a machine to comb it, and then beaten into place with a long stick. Cotton can also be bought on the roll. Although many purists prefer natural cotton there is one strong disadvantage, that after use it starts to knot up. In the Middle East it is not a problem if you take your quilt to the neighbourhood quilter and mattress-stuffer and he gives you a fresh filling every year, but for the busy Western housewife it is impractical to open the quilt and restuff it. In Scandinavia, at the turn of the century, they used wool. This was extremely warm, although rather heavy and the work involved in preparing it is quite extensive.

I use synthetic fibre. It is sometimes called acrylic and sometimes polyester. It comes on long rolls of 30 to 40 metres and is usually about 140 cm wide. It is very easy to lace layers together with a large running stitch if you should need it wider, and it is washable, light, and yet warm and easy to work with. The needle slides through it as if it were air. This fibre comes in several different weights, according to how heavy it is. If you want a very thick quilt you could use a 5 or 6 oz. If you buy a thinner weight and want it thicker, it is easy to double the layers.

The backing

I used to use a cheap cream-coloured muslin. It was inexpensive and came in large widths so that saved me the time and bother of having to sew panels together to make the backing. The only problem with this material was that it shrank up to 15% so it had to be washed and shrunk beforehand. I grew very tired of washing and ironing 40 to 50 metres of this material each time, so I started using a fine printed cloth to match the patchwork design. It was more expensive, but it was worth it.

In Sri Lanka I use fine Swiss sheeting for the back. I usually can get away with using either beige for the brown-toned quilts, light blue for the blue tones, and pink for the rest. The sheeting is what bed sheets are usually made out of and is fairly heavy, large in width and also rather easy to work with. Once again, as with all parts of quilting, you are left with a large measure of freedom to choose what is available and easy to work with.

Middle Eastern quilting technique (mainly by hand)

The first thing you have to do if you are going to quilt is to lay the finished top on a table or the floor, and measure the backing to be exactly the same size as the top. Then pin around the sides, and with a sewing machine close three sides completely and part of the way down each side of the fourth side (see fig. 100). Then turn the layers inside out and place the stuffing on top of the two outside layers (inside out) and cut that to be exactly the same size. Turn the corners as shown in figure 101 and roll it up evenly, and rather tightly, leaving an open section at one end (fig. 102). Then put your hands into the opening and pull the entire piece back through the open section. Pick it up by the two top corners, making sure that you have all three layers in each hand, and then shake it out, much as you would a duvet.

Once you have turned the quilt, and smoothed out the three layers, making sure the filler is evenly spaced, you should then immediately pin the opening shut and sew it with an invisible hem stitch.

Using a darning needle, or other large needle, and a thimble around the middle finger, quilt the layers by sewing around the frame. It can be done on a large table or on the floor. The first stitching around the outside frame is very important because this holds the filling securely and neatly in place.

After sewing the outside frame, sew down the middle crossways and then lengthways, to make sure the filling does not creep to one side or the other. Then continue the lines of stitching from top to bottom and side to side. The lines can be as wide apart as 15 cm.

American quilting technique (by hand)

There are several variations on the American method of quilting, but basically it consists of stretching the top, filling and bottom layer like a sandwich, and then tacking the layers together in more or less the same way you would cut across a pie or a cake, across, up and down and then diagonally.

For this you can use a small quilting hoop (fig. 103) or a frame (fig. 104), blocking off a small area of about a foot (30 cm), quilting that area, and then moving another foot. For this method it is best to use a fine

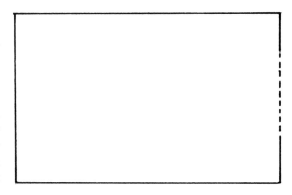

100 *How to turn a quilt*
101 *Folding corners on turning quilt*

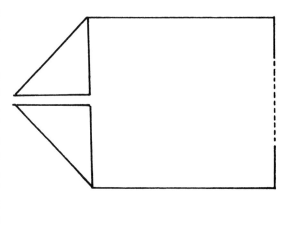

102 *Rolling-turning quilt*

but heavy quilting thread together with a smaller needle and a thimble. Unlike the Arabic system, American quilting demands overall stitching, sometimes even smothering the block in intricate flower or leaf designs. When you finish the American method the sides are still open. You must then trim the three layers and attach a binding along the outside of the quilt.

63

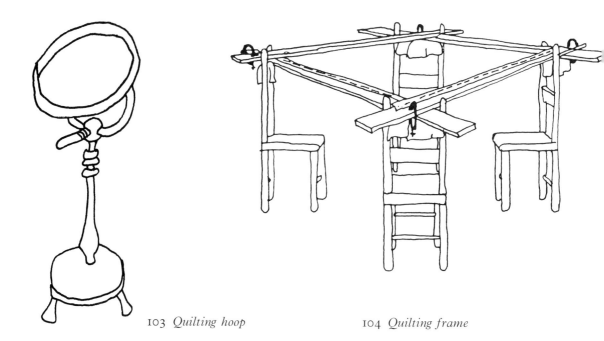

103 *Quilting hoop*　　　　104 *Quilting frame*

Joan Zinni Lask method

There is another technique which is similar to the American method, but it is much more practical and easy to do. In the absence of another name I will call it after the lady who taught it to me, and to a generation of British women in her quilt classes in London. Finish a row of patchwork, but do not attach it to the other rows as I have just described. Instead, cut a layer of filling and a layer of backing, and quilt just that row. Then do the same process for the next rows. When you have finished all the rows, attach the front two layers, either by machine or by hand, and the back layer you fold over and close with a hemming stitch done by hand. If you prefer to work block by block, the exact same process can still be done.

Possible quilting stitches

Figure 105 shows some quilting stitches which could be used in either technique. If you do a plain modern quilt using the Arabic technique, these stitches could also be used to decorate the plain area. You can mark the material with pencil through a transparent perforated sheet of paper (the early Americans used cinnamon) or by merely scratching the material with a needle, which can be easily seen against the light. The stitches may be any size, but should be uniform in length. An irregular stitch does not look good. There are some fanatics of the American technique who insist that there must be 12 or 15 stitches per inch, or that one must use a particular angle when sewing down through the cloth, and another equally eccentric angle when sewing up through the material; again, my advice is do what you feel comfortable with.

Machine-quilting

You should prepare the quilt for machine-stitching in the same way that you would prepare the quilt in the American method. Lay the three layers out as if it were a sandwich, and then tack all three together. Start in the middle and quilt across from top to bottom or from side to side.

The trick of machine-quilting is to guide the quilt through the machine with both hands flat and feed the quilt into the machine. If it is very big and bulky it is a

64

105 *Quilting stitches*

good idea to have a second person behind the machine, pulling it through, and helping you to support the weight.

When you have finished the quilting, sew the three layers closed along the edges and then clip the excess. There is usually a little wastage, especially from the back layer as you must leave a certain excess in order to be able to quilt.

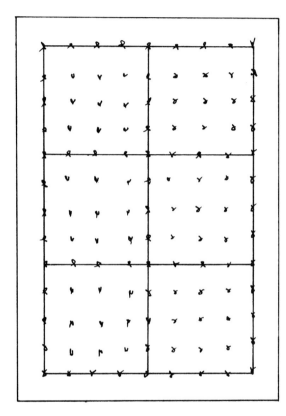

Tie quilting

This is a special type of quilting (fig. 106). The layers may be prepared either in the American or the Middle Eastern method. For the quilting, take a bright, colourful thread, and push the needle through all three layers, coming back through to the top, very near the same place. Cut the thread and tie it into a double knot making sure that part of the colourful thread is still visible on top. The texture and colour enhances different design effects, and is a fast and painless method of quilting.

Finishing off

When you have finished, either hand- or machine-quilting, the last stage is to sew the binding on. I usually sew a $6\frac{1}{2}$ cm binding strip matching the material used in the outer frame. Sew this onto the back side of the quilt and turn the tape over, pinning it into place before sewing.

Non-quilted coverlet

If you do not want to go to the trouble of quilting your top piece, you could merely sew on the filling or backing, either directly as with a pillow case, or using a binding.

106 *Tie quilting*

4

Modern versions of traditional patchwork

Many Americans feel somewhat religious about the names of traditional patchwork blocks and become highly offended if they are changed or altered. But some patterns have always had several names, being called one thing in one part of the country and something completely different elsewhere. They can be colourful and are suggestive of folklore, but I think patchwork is just as much a contemporary art, as well as a traditional one; hence I have renamed quilts to suggest my environment.

There are many varieties of traditional patterns some of which are described in this chapter. Many are old with a long history, others I have made up, but they fit well into the traditional vocabulary and on the whole I have chosen the ones which I feel best fit our modern tools and material.

Three different types of patchwork patterns are dealt with here: first, patterns which are made from one cutting piece; second, patterns built up by blocks; and finally appliqué patterns.

One-piece patterns

The easiest pattern to start off with is the square: you don't have to worry about tricky corners and difficult matching seams. Since the pattern piece is all the same, the pattern is achieved by the different arrangements and use of colour. With the square

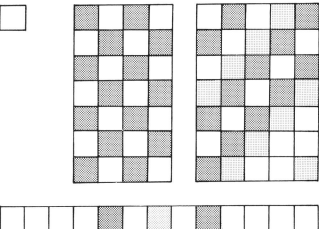
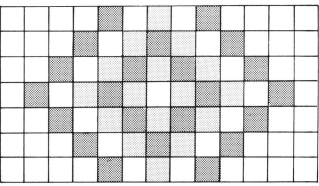

107 *The square*

(fig. 107) there are three different possibilities. The most popular is called Round the World. It is also possible to arrange the colours in a stepped pattern or as a checkerboard. The popularity of this pattern shows that a design need not be complex to be

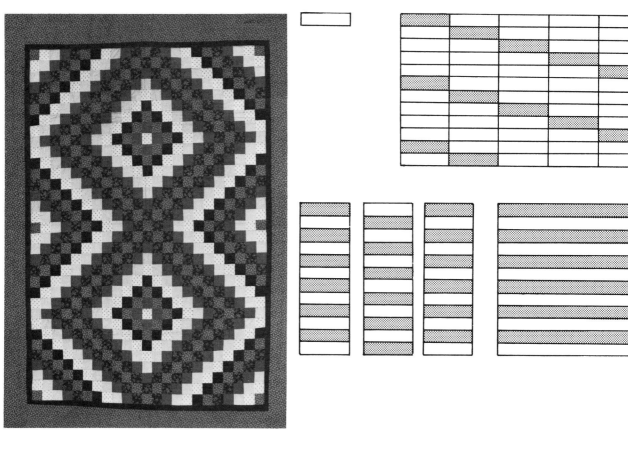

108 *Double Round the World (above left)*
109 *The rectangle (above right)*
110 *Strips (right)*

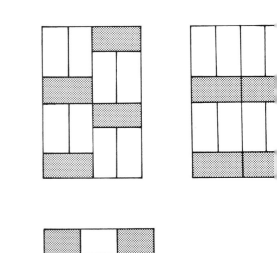

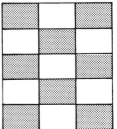

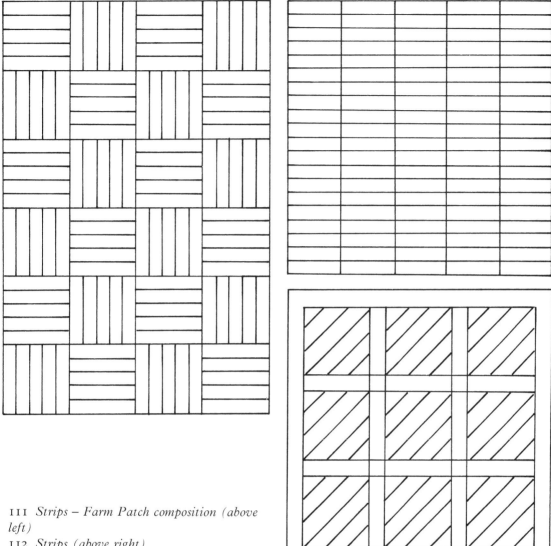

111 *Strips – Farm Patch composition (above left)*

112 *Strips (above right)*

113 *Trapezoids (right)*

successful. Figure 108 shows a quilt made in a double Round the World pattern, using fairly small blocks. Once again the patterns may be made more simple or more complex by merely enlarging or decreasing the size of the blocks.

The rectangle (fig. 109) is another fairly simple pattern to start off with, and once again there are different possibilities of design, depending on how the colour is used.

Strips are another possibility for one-pattern design. Depending on the material and colour you choose, this design can look very traditional and old fashioned, or modern and bold (figs 110, 111 and 112). Grandmother's Step (colour plate 5) shows a very traditional treatment of the pattern. The first piece of each block is always black and it runs through the pattern the way a step would. It also lends a more dramatic air to the traditionally gay quilt. Colour

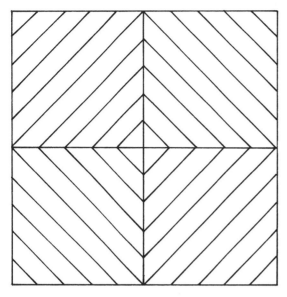

114 *Trapezoids (above)*
115 *Purity (below)*

plate 6 shows strips used in a more modern way. The plain colours and the white background give it a colourful simplicity.

Trapezoids are also frequently used as pattern pieces, although cutting these out is more difficult (figs 113 and 114). Once cut, piecing the quilt together is fairly quick. Figure 115 shows a quilt using elongated trapezoids. The border is navy-blue and its various shades of blue and turquoise reminded me of mountain water so I called it Purity.

Figure 116 shows some of the different types of one-pattern design which can be made with triangles. You can vary the size of the sides of the triangle to give different effects, although the easiest to work with on a large scale is the equilateral triangle because its sides are all the same length. Figure 117 shows the equilateral triangle completed.

Diamonds are other pattern pieces which, although difficult to work with, present great design possibilities. Baby Blocks (fig. 54) shows what it is like completed. I find it very hard to sew with because it involves sewing four corners, which can be tedious, but if you take it step by step, perhaps only setting a target of three or four rows a day, it will eventually be worth the trouble (fig. 118).

Rhomboids (fig. 119) are the last single-cutting piece I will mention. There are many possibilities of using this pattern for modern design as e.g., in Waves (fig. 63).

Patterns using blocks

An easy way to start making blocks is to begin with squares. Figures 120–125 show some possibilities. The 9-Patch is shown completed in figure 5. Figure 121 shows the 16-Patch. Figures 124 and 125 taken together make the pattern Irish Chain (colour plate 3). These patterns can be placed alone afterwards or, as shown in the two completed pieces of patchwork, interspersed with plain or patterned blocks to emphasize the patterns.

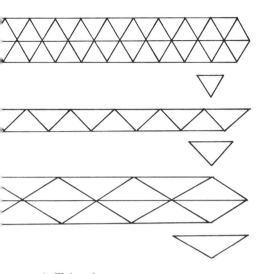

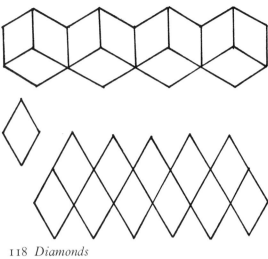

116 *Triangles*
117 *Triangle quilt*

118 *Diamonds*

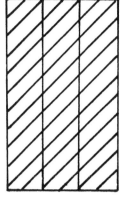

119 *Rhomboids*
120 *4-Patch*

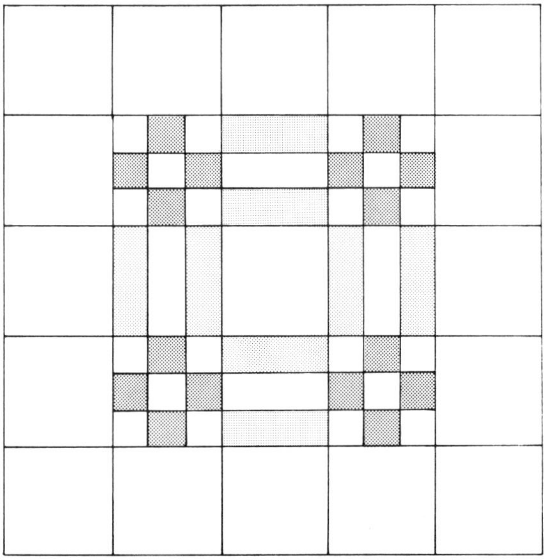

121 *16-Patch (above left)*
122 *Album patch (above right)*
123 *9-Patch version 2 (right)*
124 *Irish Chain block 1 (below left)*
125 *Irish Chain block 2 (below right)*

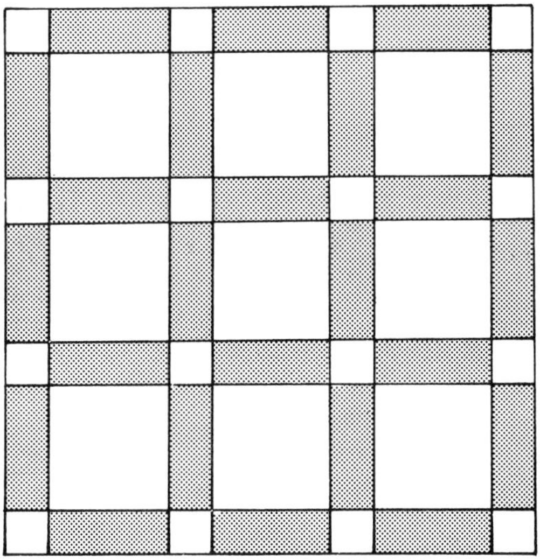

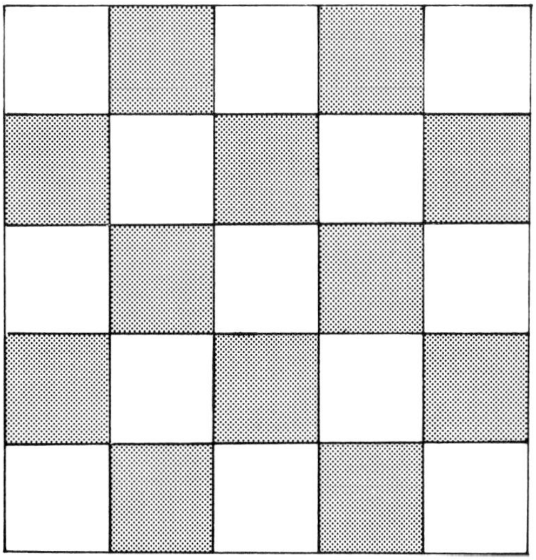

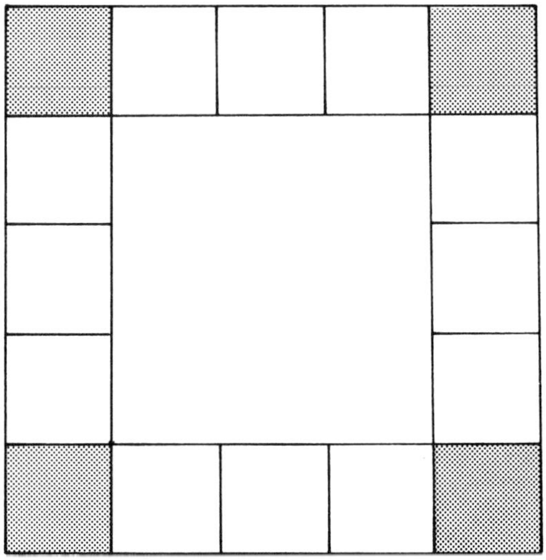

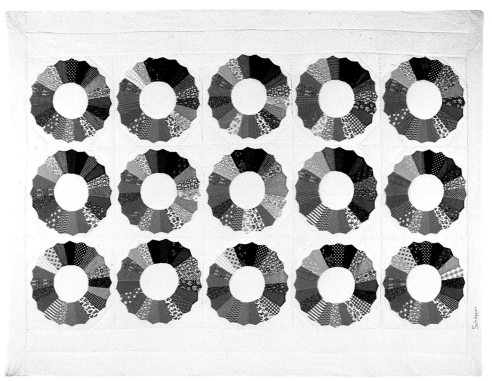

Dresden Plate

Mexican Rose

Irish Chain

Footpaths

Graduation

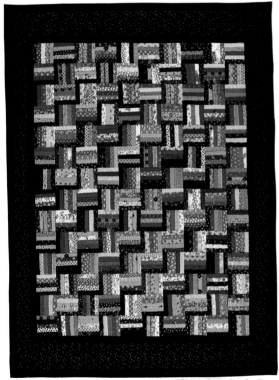

Grandmother's Step

Sailboats

Schenzer

Day and Night

Study in Lights

Blue Motion

Triangle quilt

Necktie

Spring Pattern

Fall Pattern

Sampler quilt

Mixing squares and triangles

Mixing squares and triangles results in satisfying patterns but is more complicated. Figures 126 and 127, taking half dark light and the other half light dark, result in the pattern I call Positive Negative (fig. 52). Figure 128, basically the same but with the addition of squares in the middle of the diamond, is shown as a Russian quilt in figures 16, 17 and 18. In figure 129 another set of triangles is added and when placed

126 *Positive-Negative piece 1*
127 *Positive-Negative piece 2*

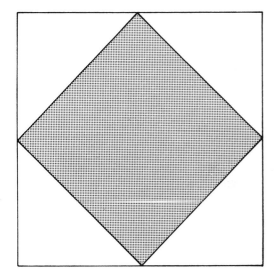

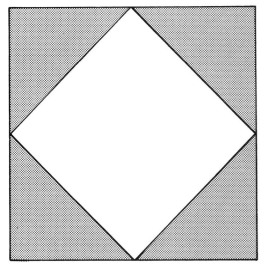

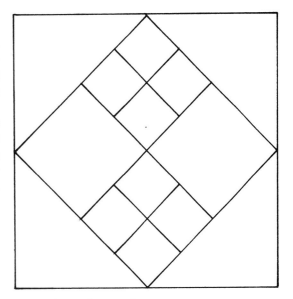

128 *Diamond 4-patch*

together it is spaced with a plain square of alternating colour so forming the Puzzle quilt (fig. 130).

Jacob's Ladder and Goose in the Corner are more complex possibilities of combining triangles and squares (figs 131 and 132).

The smaller and larger version of the Album quilt is signed in the middle as in the manner of the gift quilt. I mentioned this tradition in chapter 1, where several people made a quilt, each one signing the block she had made as a souvenir (figs 133 and 134). This pattern could be a very typical gift quilt.

White House Steps (fig. 135) is a pattern which can be seen in figure 25 in what I renamed Homage to Vasarely because of its similarity to his painting.

Figures 136 and 137 are easy patterns to do. I got the idea from the tiles on the streets in Lisbon and other smaller Portuguese cities, where there are beautiful mosaic streets made of a cream-coloured stone alternating with a yellowish colour.

The inspiration for figure 138 came from South America and is called Ojo de Dios or Eye of God. It is customary in South America for poor people to make crosses for

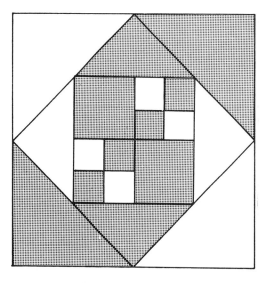

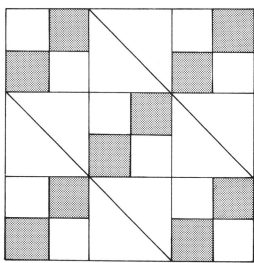

129 *Puzzle block*
130 *Puzzle quilt*

131 *Jacob's Ladder*
132 *Goose in the Pond*

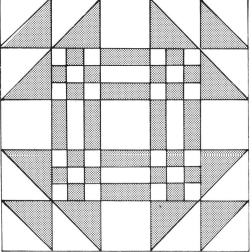

74

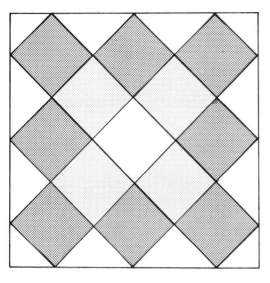

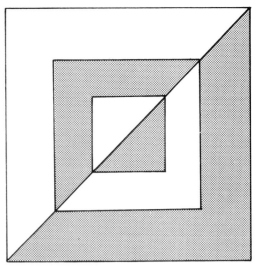

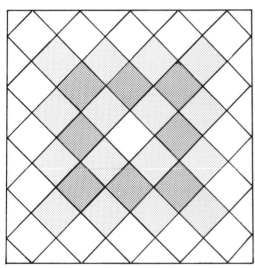

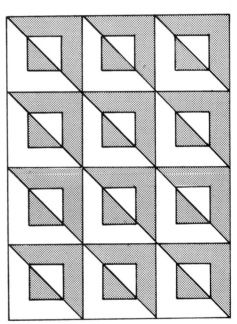

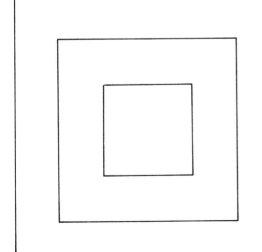

133 *Album quilt 1 (top left)*
134 *Album quilt 2 (centre left)*
135 *White House Steps (left)*
136 *Variation on Porto (top right)*
137 *Variation on Porto (centre right)*

75

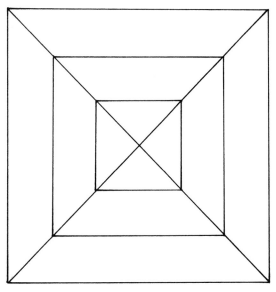

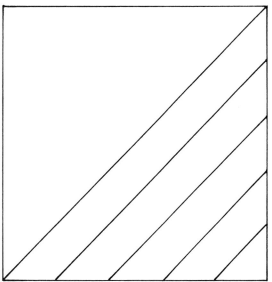

religious ceremonies out of twigs and then bind them with brightly coloured wool or cotton. The final shape is similar to this pattern.

Figure 139 shows the pattern Trapeze, and the completed quilt using this pattern is shown in figure 140. It could easily be made less sombre by using pastel colours, rather than as here with navy-blue, shades of rust and medium blue. I call my version Rainfall because it reminds me of rainy winter days.

138 *Ojo di Dios (top)*
139 *Trapeze (bottom)*
140 *Rainfall (right)*

Figures 141–144 show other interesting possibilities of design. Figure 145, Porto, is shown completed in figure 67b.

Triangles can be used in an interesting way (figs 146–155). One of my favourites is the half triangle (fig. 146). It is simple and uniform and, depending on the use of colour, the impression can be changed completely. Colour plate 7, which I call Sailboats, is made of fresh shades of green and blue on a cream background and reminds me of a summer's day.

141 *Diagonal (top left)*
142 *Bull's Eye (bottom left)*
143 *Cat and Mouse (top right)*
144 *Stripes and Squares (bottom right)*

145 *Porto (top left)*
146 *Half triangle (bottom left)*
147 *Bowtie/Necktie (top right)*
148a & b *Spider's Web (left)*
149 *Flying Geese (opposite top)*
150 *Sawtooth (opposite centre)*
151 *Pinwheel (opposite bottom)*
152 *Red, White and Blue (opposite top right)*
153 *Sunflowers (opposite below right)*

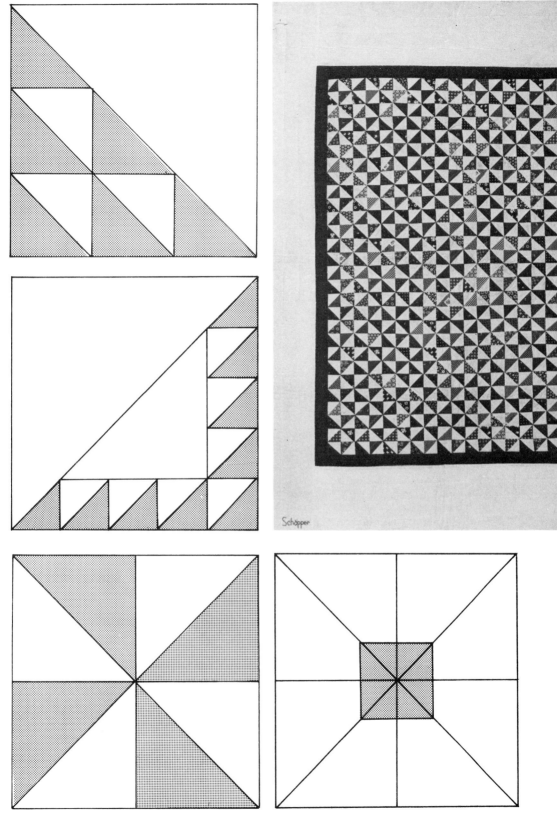

Schöpper

79

154 *Flying Geese (top left)*
155 *Bull's Eye (bottom left)*
156 *Autumn Leaves (top right)*
157 *Mexican Rose (bottom right)*

Colour plate 8, which I call Day and Night, was made in Dusseldorf one winter when we didn't see the sun for months and the nights were black and the days were grey.

Figure 147 is the pattern for a quilt I have made many times, in different colours. I call it Necktie or Bowtie (fig. 45). Figure 148a, which is divided hexagonally, is ex-

tremely difficult to do. The lines of colour are hard to keep straight in a large quilt, and all the small corners are tedious to sew but the finished quilt is rewarding (fig. 148b).

Flying Geese (fig. 149), or Triangle quilt and Sawtooth (fig. 150) are attractive when finished because of the repeated uniformity of the design. Pinwheel (fig. 151) has already been shown in figure 83 as a stark, serious quilt spaced with white blocks called The Vikings, because the decoration resembles the figurehead which the Vikings used to have on their ships. Figure 152 shows a completely different version of the

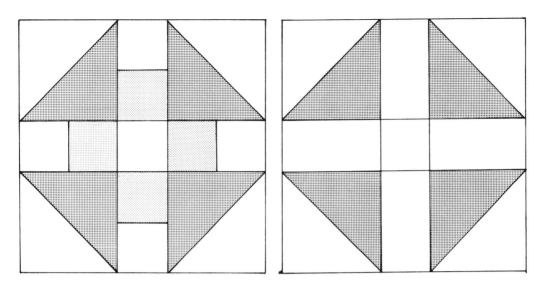

158 *Churn-Dash*
(above left)
159 *Star (above right)*

160 *Vilnius Pillow*

81

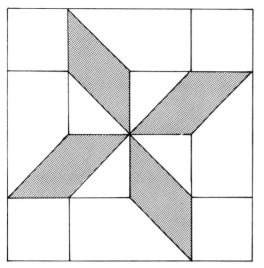
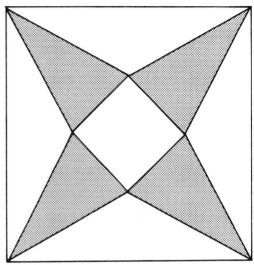
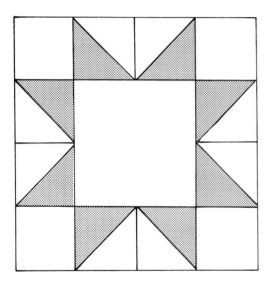
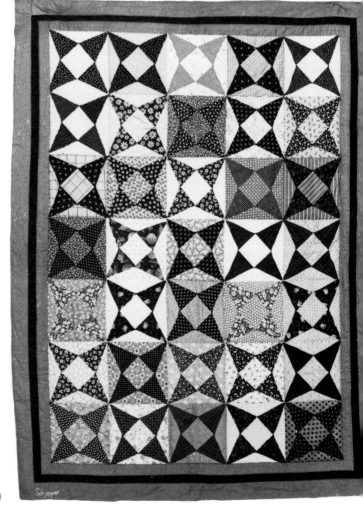

161 *Windmill (top left)*
162 *Little Star (bottom left)*
163 *Black Star (top right)*
164 *World Without End (bottom right)*

82

same pattern. It is much smaller and the centre is in red and navy-blue alternating with cream-coloured grey cloth so the quilt has a much fresher, juvenile look, or even a somewhat patriotic feel as it reflects the red, white and blue colours in some flags. In fact I have called the quilt Red, White and Blue.

Figure 153 was an attempt to geometrify the sunflower. Although I made the quilt out of various shades of plain yellow with a brown centre and separated it with an olive-green diagonal border, it was not what I was hoping for and I never finished it, but perhaps you can do something with the idea.

Figure 154, Flying Geese, lends itself to either traditional or modern interpretations. In figure 39 a traditional yet sophisticated interpretation is done in black-and-white printed fabrics. Figure 89 shows a more old-fashioned olive and beige rendition and figure 224 shows a strong red, white and blue three-dimensional approach. Figure 223 shows the same pattern made as a mobile.

Figures 156–169 make up what I call the Star Patterns because of their resemblance to various types of stars. The pattern in figure 156 is shown as the finished quilt of beige and olive colours in figure 10. The pattern Mexican Rose (fig. 157) can be seen in a finished quilt in colour plate 2. The patterns shown in figures 158 and 159 can be seen worked as a pillow in figure 160 in cream, beige, olive and rust.

Figure 162, Little Star, is shown completed in figure 50. It is worked in red-printed fabric on a pale cream background.

Figure 163 shows the block for a quilt I made when there was heavy bombing in Beirut. The background is strong blues and turquoise and the stars are in various shades of black, hence its name, Black Star (fig. 164). The quilt conveys a sense of destruction and tension. But of course other colours would completely change the effect.

Figure 165 shows a pattern similar to that shown in figure 166 where I used strong contrasting colours. The design would also

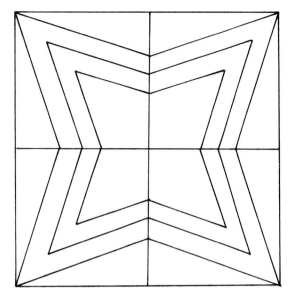

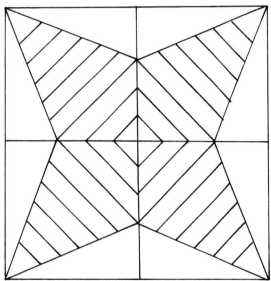

165 *Star (top)*
166 *Rocky Road to Kansas (bottom)*

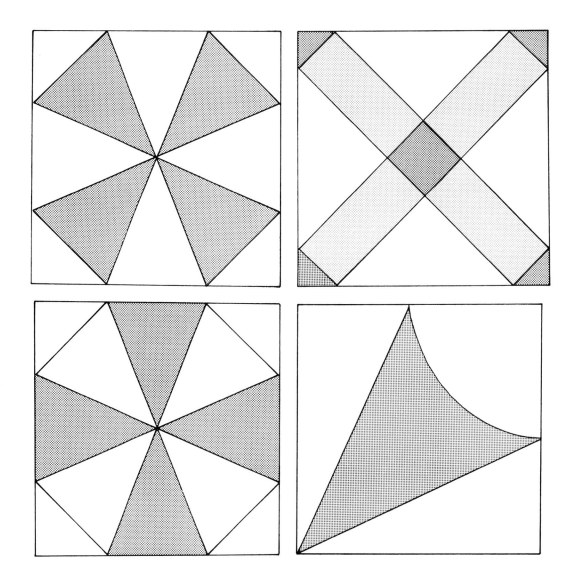

85

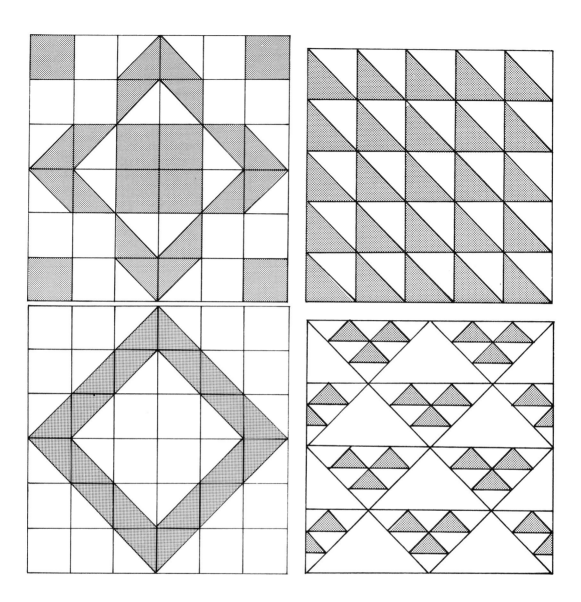

be attractive in lighter shades.

Figures 167 and 168 show the two types of block necessary for Kaleidoscope (fig. 66a) and figure 169 shows the block layout for Study in Lights, the finished quilt shown in colour plate 9.

Figure 170, Kaleidoscope, is shown made in a brown and red printed material in figure 171. This was a difficult patchwork to do, particularly in keeping the colour patterns straight, but the final effect is very striking.

Figures 172–192 show a variety of blocks

172 *Cat in the Corner (top left)*
173 *Diamond (bottom left)*
174 *Day and Night (top right)*
175 *Flying Geese (bottom right)*

86

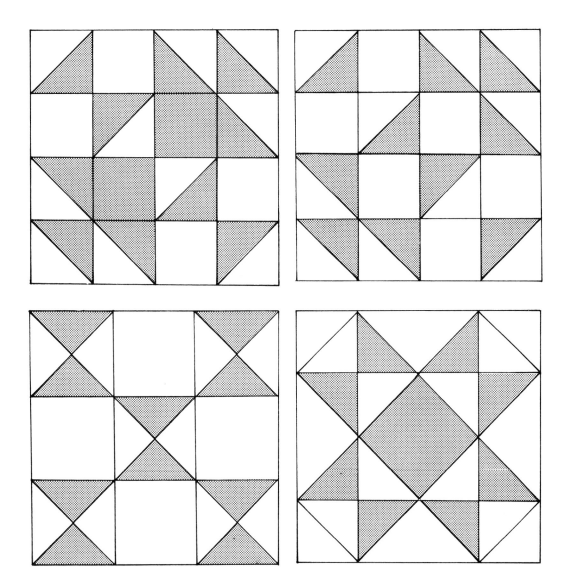

which can be made with the same basic triangular pieces. Different colours and colour combinations will give different effects. In Pink Pansy (fig. 188), which is a very similar pattern to the previous ones, I managed to achieve the effects with white blocks.

Spring and Fall (fig. 187, colour plates 13 and 14) and Footpaths (fig. 189, colour plate 4) also use triangular blocks rather effectively. There are many possibilities for using simple geometric shapes to make unique and distinctive patchwork.

176 *Old Ladies' Puzzle (top left)*
177 *Letter X (bottom left)*
178 *Turning Star (top right)*
179 *Squares and triangles (bottom right)*

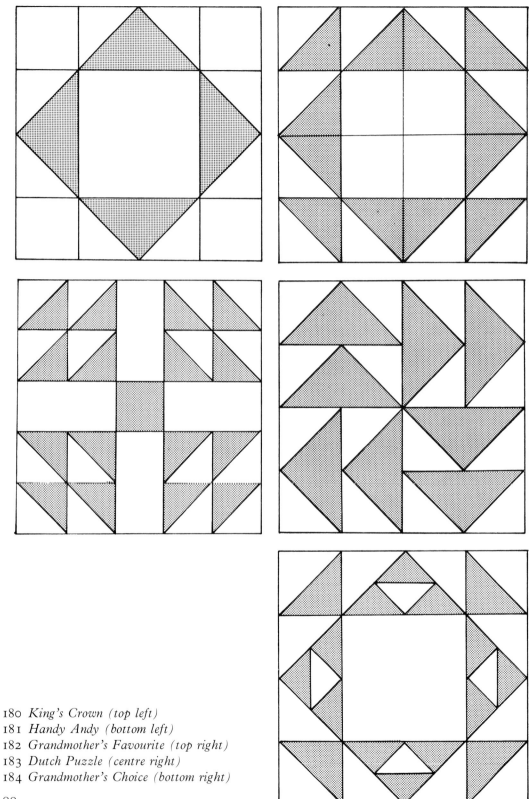

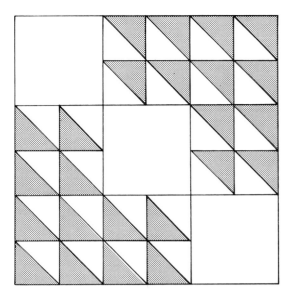

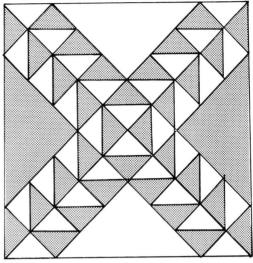

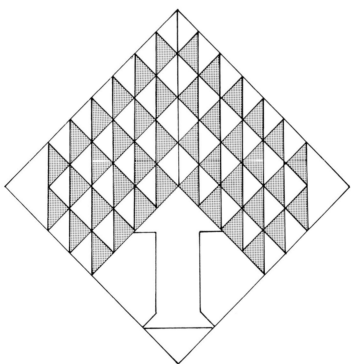

185 *Flying Geese Variation (top left)*
186 *Spring Pattern (top right)*
187 *Christmas Tree (bottom)*

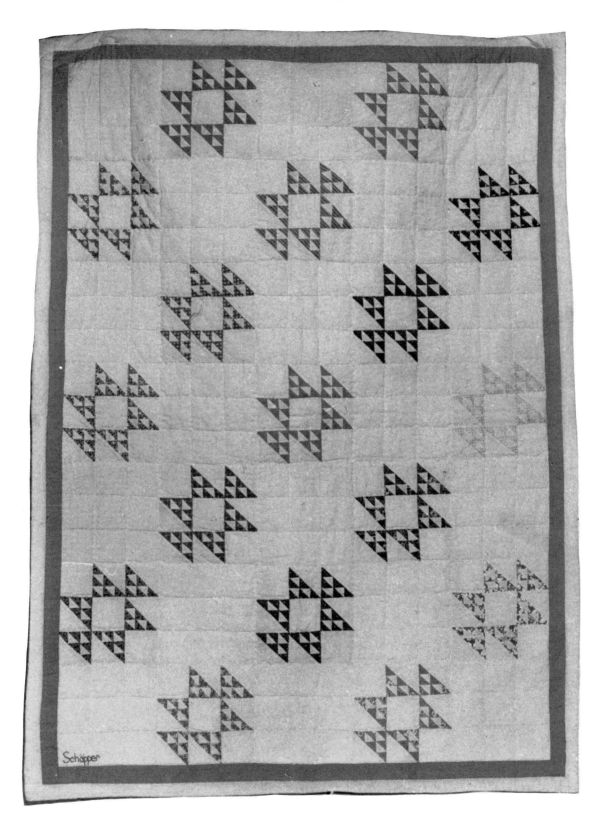

Schäpper

90

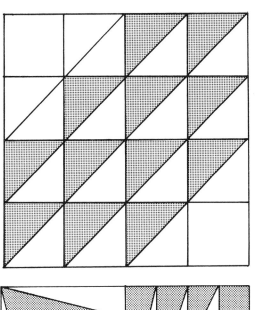

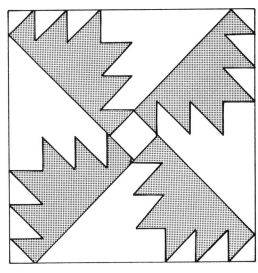

188 *Pink Pansy (opposite)*
189 *Footpaths (top left)*
190 *Palm (bottom left)*
191 *Kansas Trouble (top right)*
192 *Diamond (centre right)*
193 *Lily (bottom right)*

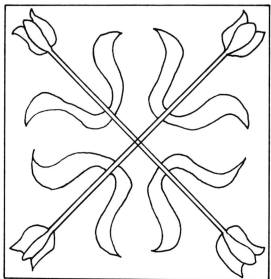

194 *Bridal Wreath (above left)*
195 *Tulip (above right)*

Appliqué blocks

Appliqué may involve some piecing together of the blocks on the machine but the piece should then be sewn by hand onto the background. Figures 193–201 show several varieties of flowers and rounded figures which have been done like this.

Figures 202 and 203 show ideas for baby quilts. Figure 204 shows the completed baby quilt.

Star of David (fig. 205) was the first quilt I ever made, and can be seen completed in

196 *Tulip (below left)*
197 *Flower Wreath (below left)*

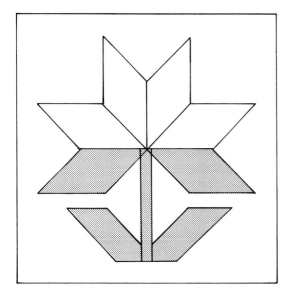

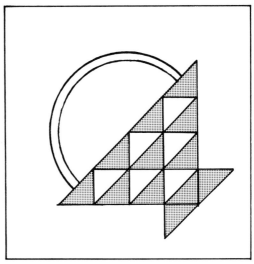

figure 55. Crazy quilt (fig. 206) is a fun way to use up all the irregular small scraps and odd-shaped pieces (fig. 34). It is easily done. Baste the pieces into place on a background, turning under the edges where necessary, and after laying out the entire block, fasten the pieces with a decorative embroidery stitch.

Figure 207, The Tree, was my first original design and can be seen completed in figure 56. Dresden Plate (fig. 208) is an easy design to begin on and can be seen completed in colour plate 1. Bluebells (fig.

198 *Poinsetta (above left)*
199 *Bread Basket (above right)*

200 *Circle with Cross (below left)*
201 *Robbing Peter to Pay Paul (below right)*

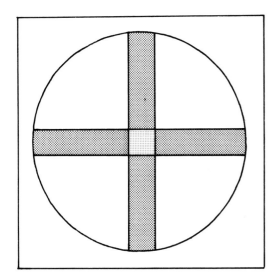

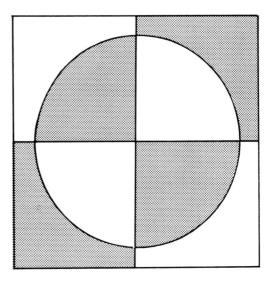

202 *Bird*

203 *Lion*

204 *Complete baby quilt*

94

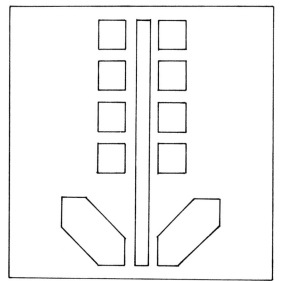

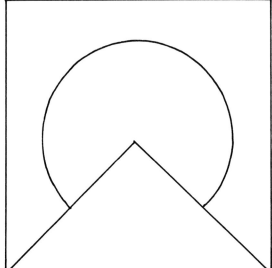

209 *Bluebells*

209) is an appliquéd quilt I designed after sitting in a garden in Switzerland and looking at the bluebells (fig. 60). Figure 210 shows Moon over the Mountain, completed in figure 51. Fans (figs 211a and 211b) is done in beige with a decorative embroidery stitch along the outside rounded edge which is also in beige.

I worked the same pattern in bright, yellow-printed fabrics so it looked like the rising sun, and called it English Sunrise.

There are numerous possibilities for appliqué and the ideas are quite easy to develop, from plants, flowers, trees or literally anything in your environment.

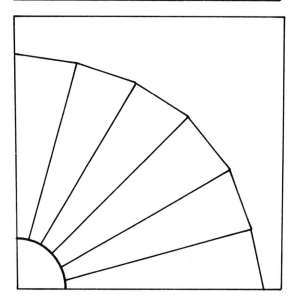

210 *Moon Over the Mountain (top right)*
211a & b *Fans (above and opposite)*

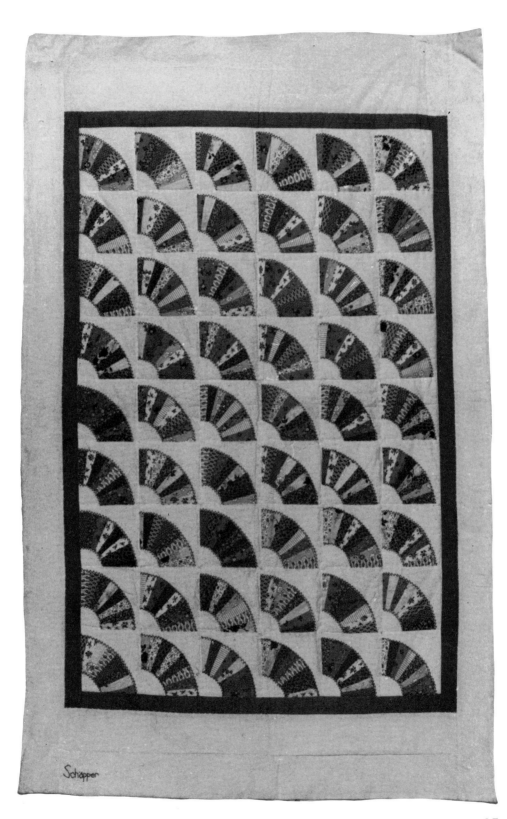

Schäpper

5
Colour

Colour is so important that it rates a chapter by itself. Even in the most beautiful technical work, and the most fascinating design, if the colour is not well chosen, the quilt will be worthless. On the other hand, colour can also save a weak design and make it attractive. Colour fascinates people: I have watched people enter a room with colourful quilts on display, and they break into a smile. It is one of the things in life, like music, which has the ability to move our emotions. It is said that mentally ill or seriously depressed people will often wear black or even go so far as to paint their walls black at home.

Certain colours are considered serious or businesslike. If a man were to wear a pink suit to a business conference, he would be judged as less than serious. But in different cultures of the world colours symbolize different things. In India and Sri Lanka white is worn for mourning. In the Catholic Church, green is the colour of hope, and red the colour of suffering or martyrdom. It is traditional for baby girls to wear light pink and baby boys light blue, but I find that children prefer brightly coloured fabrics.

One of the strongest influences on our feelings about colour are the cultures we grow up in.

Our natural surroundings, for instance plants and vegetation life, can have some influence on how people feel about colours.

I have found that Scandinavians love pale colours, whites and beige, such as the colours in Study in Lights (colour plate 9). If you travel to Sweden in the winter you can drive miles and miles through snow-covered farm land with the only colour being the red barns and golden cat tails.

The French seem to love blue, and France is surrounded by beautiful blue ocean which they love to visit. It is possible to sell pastel colours in the coastal regions of the USA but in the mid-West, Nebraska, Kansas and Iowa, people generally prefer earth colours which reflect the colour of the land on which they live. Bright colours in what I call the rainbow-scheme sell better in the Mediterranean countries where the light is very bright.

Light has a lot to do with colour interpretation. I have made quilts in light pastels in tropical Sri Lanka and been very disappointed that they are so dull and uninteresting, then brought them to my office in Copenhagen and opened the box to be surprised at the warm interesting colour combination. While living in India I made beautiful bright quilts and the reverse happened. I brought them to the quiet light of Copenhagen and the colours were so bold they hurt the eyes.

Dress fashion also plays an important part in our acceptance of various colour combinations. When I was growing up in rural

Michigan it was considered shocking to put blue and green together. Pink and red was considered an equally disgusting combination. Now these colours, as fashion combinations, are an accepted part of our everyday vocabulary.

In Denmark many clothes are imported from India, where a favourite colour combination is murky purple with red. Quilts in these colours are likewise popular, whereas in France, for example, the same colour combination is considered morose. Olive-green is a favourite colour in Austria and Germany where the olive-green Loden coats and suits are still in vogue.

Magazines and advertising can often influence our preferences for colour combinations, although it is an unconscious influence.

Colour suggestions

I would like to offer some different suggestions about the way colour can be used, based on what I have learned living in several different cultures.

The surprise

One interesting method is to put in a surprise colour, or one you would not expect. In a quilt of browns and beiges, a pink is slightly out of line and adds interest to the quilt.

In Blue Motion (colour plate 10), the whole design comes from the use of blues. The green is a surprise and cannot be ignored, but in my opinion that is the reason for the success of the quilt.

Study in Lights (colour plate 9) contrasts the calm beiges and creams with red. The red is unexpected and makes it both sweet and strong. In Day and Night (colour plate 8), the black and grey are unexpectedly interrupted by the sharp yellow. Once I made a quilt of dark burgundy, pumpkin orange and dark red, and put the last border in apple green, which made it less sober and more dramatic.

When planning your quilts, try experimenting by introducing a colour which does not immediately seem to go with the rest of the colours in the quilt.

Primary colours

Using the basic primary colours of red, yellow, blue and green, or red, white and blue, or red, yellow and green, gives a strong youthful appearance to any quilt. It is almost as strong as pop-art and is well suited to children and their environment. I have been disappointed whenever I have tried to use these simple colours myself but several Scandinavian designers have become well known worldwide for their excellent use of primary colours against white.

White or cream background

Although white adds a strong contrast to any colour, off-white or cream tends to add a softening, more romantic look. Combining cream, or off-white, with light pink or egg-shell yellow has a much softer effect than combining cream with navy or dark green. In general the closer the shades are in hue and depth, the softer the look.

Mixing in black

Although black is not a commercially popular colour, perhaps because of funereal associations, it is an interesting colour to use in a quilt. It adds a bit of mystery and depth to any quilt. Black and green, or black and turquoise, black and red, or black and beige all make strong contrasts and have a lot of magnetism (see Flying Geese, fig. 39, or Day and Night, colour plate 8).

Placing like shades together

There is something intensely pleasing about placing shades in the same colour range next to each other (see Graduation, colour plate 6; and Dresden Plate, colour plate 1). You can work around the spectrum in this way, placing all the reds, greens, blues together and so on to create spectacular effects.

Mix up warm, cool and neutral colours

At school we all learned that red, yellow and orange were warm colours, blues and greens cool colours and grey and beige neutral. One of the most interesting ways of using colour is to mix them up completely, putting red and grey together, or beige and blue, or orange and blue.

Nature as inspiration

They say God is the greatest artist. If we look around at some of the things in the natural world it would be hard to argue against, and we cannot go far wrong if we copy some of these colour combinations. Study the feathers on nearly any species of bird; the colouration on animals, horses, cats; the colours of flowers or falling leaves in the autumn. Note the colours of mountains or the sky at different times of the day. Butterflies, stones, wood, rainbows, rainstorms, metals and gems all give ideas for beautiful colour combinations.

Practical application of colour rules

Talking theoretically about colour is one thing. Actually sitting down and using it is another. Let us analyse the colour combinations used in five of my quilts.

Triangle Quilt (colour plate 11)

Half of the quilt, or every other triangle, is in a dark brown. The other half is divided into ten parts. Five parts consist of beige- or white-printed fabric, giving a neutral effect. The other half, consisting of five parts, is cut equally from red, yellow, blue, green and pink material, giving the quilt enough colour to be interesting, yet allowing enough quiet colours to keep it from being too nervous.

The type of material is also divided into

three types. I use about 20 per cent plain material, in brown, beige or one of the other colours. Twenty per cent is material with a bold or large pattern such as a flower or leaves, but most of the quilt, or roughly 60 per cent, is made up of small patterned material (see fig. 212). Using a lot of fabric with a small pattern tends to make the design nervous, too much plain fabric makes it rather modern and dramatic, too much large pattern and the overall patchwork pattern doesn't come through.

212 *Types of prints*

Bowtie (colour plate 12)

Although Bowtie looks like a typical rag-quilt, or what is commonly referred to as a 'grandmother's-quilt', there is nevertheless a system behind it. I divide the colour scheme into ten parts: brown, blue, green, purple, pink, red, yellow, orange, neutral and black. You can then take an equal number of each colour. I normally weight the darker ones a little more and, for instance, instead of ten parts of each colour, I would pair them and take fifteen parts brown, and five yellow; fifteen blue, and five orange. I don't like bright colours, and this is a formula which can be used to tame the effect. I use the same division of the fabric into plain, small-patterned and large-patterned prints. I like to tame the design by using a small plain black border, and here is one example where the colour is so strong that the black does not make it too sombre.

Use only materials you like. Don't think you can take any old fabrics and, put together, they will suddenly become beautiful. Twenty ugly fabrics make an ugly quilt.

Spring Pattern (colour plate 13)

I would like to explain the two-colour combinations I have developed for this quilt. The light blue in the pattern has a bit of white for the flowers and orange for the centre of the flower, and that is why I chose to co-ordinate it with cream and orange. It is nice to buy material with two or three highlights in it to bring in colours you would otherwise probably not think of. Although most printed fabrics have two colours, any time you are lucky enough to find a fabric with more colours, try it out. One word of caution. There should be at least one predominant colour in each material. Blur your eyes and see if there is a colour which stands out. It is hard to make a pattern with a nondescript colour scheme.

Fall Pattern (colour plate 15)

The contrast of the warm and the neutral colours, divided into six red and six brown fabrics with an equal number of pieces taken from each fabric, provides the balance for this quilt.

The Pineapple Quilt (fig. 214)

This quilt is made of six large squares. The block is made from the centre outwards, by attaching narrow bands, first dark, in this case brown, and then light, here beige. I took ten beiges and ten browns and divided them, cutting an equal number of each piece from each material. The most important thing is always to keep the balance of material so the design looks like it has been formed at random.

Autumn Leaves (fig. 10)

I have made this pattern in three different colour schemes, and it has so greatly changed the overall effect that I would like to mention each in turn.

213 *Fiesta Mexicana*

Schopper

214 *Pineapple
quilt (left)*
215 *Homage
to Joseph Albers
(opposite)*

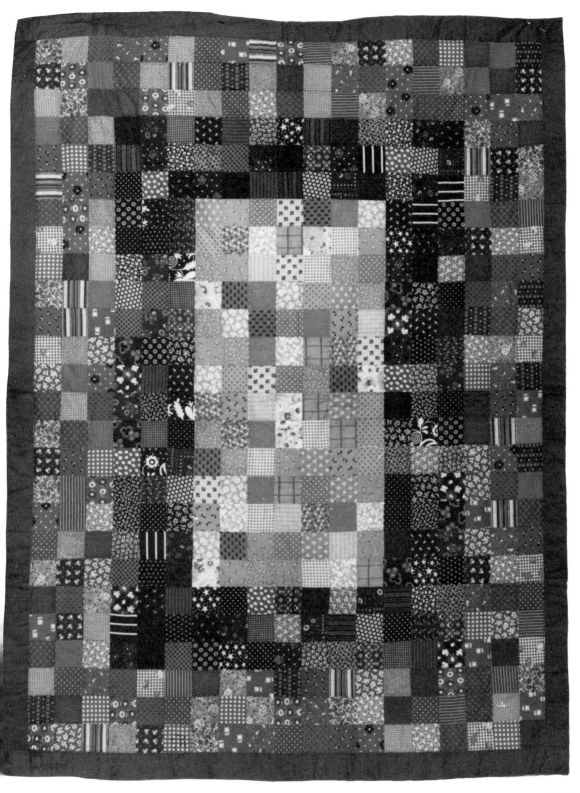

Beige-brown-burgundy

The design comprises twelve stars. On each star there are five squares and sixteen triangles, so I take twelve materials and cut one complete star from each. Four of the stars are cut in beige, four in brown, and four in burgundy. When they are placed together the colours are interchanged with another block to get the light-dark effect. Here the first border is beige and the final border is brown.

Blues

Here the blues are divided into navy-blue, mid-blue and light blue, using light blue or white for the background. With the same mathematical system as before, take twelve materials and divide them equally into the three shades of blue. I usually make a mid-blue inside border and a navy-blue outside border. It is usually a safe bet to take the darkest colour you have used inside for the last border.

Pinks

Using the same system, I divide the pinks into rose, mid-pink and light pink. I make the inner frame in light pink, and the last frame in rose.

It is interesting to see the three quilts next to each other. The beige-brown is sombre and peaceful. The blue is fresh and cool, and the pink is soft and romantic. Colour has a great effect on design.

Colour combinations

The great Bauhaus artist Joseph Albers spent his life studying the relationships between colours. He painted frames of colour, and proved that yellow had one quality when it was placed next to green, and took on a completely different quality if it was placed next to red. I have used his theories to show that materials in different colours also change depending upon what is placed next to them (fig. 215). The following is a list of some possible combinations, each of which gives quite a different effect to the main colour. Jot down next to each combination what you feel when you look at it. Is it soft? Romantic? Innocent? Disturbing? I could tell you my opinion, but yours may very likely be different, and you should start to develop your own conscious feelings and reactions to colour. We all have such a unique colour sense that it is almost as unique as our fingerprints.

Bright red	Navy
	Bright green
	Pink
	Yellow
	Brown
Burgundy	Light blue
	Beige
	Navy
	Brown
	Pink
Green	Brown
	Pink
	Beige
	Black
	White
Purple	Burgundy
	Pumpkin orange
	Yellow
	Blue
	Green
Turquoise	Burgundy
	Green
	Black
	Navy
	Purple
Beige	Brown
	Burgundy
	Pink
	Grey
	Red

6

Some approaches to modern design

I have spent a great deal of time talking about older traditional patterns. In my own work I have updated them in design, colour and finishing, but always feel that traditional designs are the only real starting point. Some of the old quilting patterns are beautiful. Interspersed with some new ideas and directions, the craft can be alive, beautiful and exciting. My favourite critical comment about my work was by a well-known textile critic writing for the *Süddeutsche Zeitung* in Munich, West Germany. She liked my work, saying 'one has to know how to use tradition without being strangled by it.'

Five ways of modernizing design

There are five different approaches towards modernizing design.
1 Using unusual materials.
2 Using new techniques and new formats.
3 Incorporating ideas from other art forms.
4 Combining other mediums and techniques.
5 Using current subject matter.
In this chapter, I would like to demonstrate each of these ideas, giving practical examples.

1 Using different materials

Although I usually use printed cotton for the major part of my designs, there are several other possibilities.

Plain-coloured cotton
Using a plain-coloured cotton often gives a dramatic, modern-art look to a design, with the textiles standing out like broad areas of paint. See Blue Motion (colour plate 10), Mouchrabieh (fig. 97), Reflections (fig. 53) and Amish Bar (fig. 216).

Denim
There is an artist in Paris who makes patchwork exclusively out of denim with white as a contrast. It is interesting to use this twentieth-century fabric with some of the old patterns.

Corduroy
I have seen an exhibition in Switzerland of an artist who makes the Log Cabin pattern in corduroy. The textures and rich, deep colours add a contemporary touch to the old pattern.

Wool
Wool is a beautiful medium to work with. The Amish, an old religious group established in colonial America by Swiss and Dutch Quakers, made all their quilts in wool. The colours and the various textures and designs on wool add a new dimension to some of the older patterns.

216 *Amish Bar*

Satin

In Lebanon and India quilts are made from satin. There are some beautiful qualities of satin for sale on the market and the inner shine of the satin adds to the patchwork effect. It is difficult to handle, and usually must be lined, but the investment of time and money is certainly worthwhile.

Silk

I have made two quilts using rough natural silk and, if you have access to silk, I highly recommend using it. Silk quilts are very much in fashion now in Italy and France. The soft colours and fine stitching make a very feminine quilt. It takes a little practice to be able to combine the colours of silk successfully. I made the mistake, in my first effort, of thinking silk has the same innocence as cotton. I took brown, red and yellow, which would have been very nice in cotton, but it was very unattractive in silk. Silk is also difficult to work with and must be lined to prevent fraying.

Lace and sequins

I found a beautiful piece of French lace, backed it with black cotton to emphasize the design, framed it in silvery blue satin and then left a large black velvet border. It was easy to make, looks elegant and I call it Innocence (fig. 217).

I made a partner for it called Corruption, which is made with the same format, but the inside piece consists of a sheet of black sequins, framed by a dark rose satin border. The outer frame is dark black velvet. It looks erotic and sexy.

Silver and gold lamé

The Amish were very strict, religious people who did not believe in using machinery; even today they prefer to drive a horse and buggy rather than use a car, and they do not have radio or television. Printed material was considered too frivolous and the women were restricted to wearing plain, sombre colours – usually dark blues, browns and black. One of the quilts they made was called Amish Diamond. I tried to take their idea to the opposite extreme by using dark colours, but intermingling them with silver lamé, rose metallic material and black nylon sparkling material. The resulting quilt (fig. 218) is one of a series I made which became known as 'disco quilts' and would indeed have looked at home in a discothèque. The London *Times* wrote about them: 'They would look out of place anywhere but on the bed of a punk rocker.' But I was very satisfied with the result and thought there could be no better way to bring quilting into our glittery disco era.

The Creation (fig. 219) tries to create a 3-D effect. The colour wheel is made in pieces and laid out as one would lay out a deck of cards in a circle. The background is beige-and-white mattress ticking, and the border in the middle is of gold lamé. The gold makes the entire piece come to life and ensures a certain undeniable vitality. It is interesting to contrast the rather sober, sultry silver in Amish Diamond to the rich, warm gold in The Creation. They both use

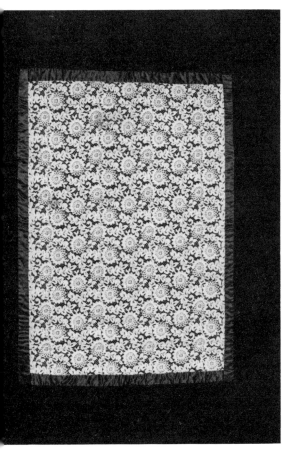 

metallic materials but, depending on how they are used, they give a very different effect.

Ribbons and labels
Ribbons and labels were used in quilt-making around the turn of the century and still offer many different varieties and shapes today which it would be interesting to experiment with. Ribbons are used in place of strips of fabric. Another idea is to take clothing labels and line them up like patchwork. Both of these could make a beautiful collage or Crazy quilt if they were decorated with an embroidery stitch.

Leather
Leather is available in several textures. It would be possible to use the softer variety in exactly the same way as you would use cotton for patchwork. The heavier type

217 *Lace quilt – Innocence (left)*
218 *Disco quilt – Amish Diamond (right)*

could also be used, but perhaps instead of sewing you could glue the patchwork onto a cardboard background. Stools and other soft furnishings have been made out of soft leather cut into patches in many African countries for centuries. The availability of so many different types and colours makes the prospect of leather as a material all the more exciting.

Newspaper and paper
Some modern artists tried making patchwork out of cut pieces of newspaper and then quilted it, supposedly to show the artificiality of our present-day culture. A quilt should last for centuries; obviously

Schäpper

108

the newspaper wouldn't. If you wanted to use the paper more constructively, you could cut out newspaper and other kinds of paper and then glue it onto a solid background. Interesting patterns for wall decoration could be made in this way.

2 Using new techniques and new formats

One of the more interesting ways to update quilting is to change some of the techniques.

Reversed seams

Some recent experiments in modern architecture reversed the traditional design order in buildings. Instead of putting the plumbing pipes and electrical tubes inside the walls as is usually done, the Pompidou Centre of Modern Art in Paris sports the pipes on the outside of the building as part of its design. The pipes are painted bright colours and wind their way up the five floors of the building. Sonia Rykel, one of France's foremost clothing designers, has recently designed her sweater collection with seams on the outside of the garments rather than the inside. She used the seams to form part of the design. I tried to do the same type of thing in a design I call Paris (fig. 220). You may recognize the design as being the same as in Study in Lights (colour plate 9). Here the under layer, consisting of three shades of beige squares, is left wrong side out so the structure of the seams shows and contributes to the design. I made the blocks separately and attached them as a lace grid by stitching the corners together and then attaching the front grid to a background. The material used is brown and olive satin, and gold lamé on the cross. I called it Paris because it is gold and glittery, and you look close and see the underworld and the seams of the city.

219 *The Creation (opposite)*
220 *Paris (above right)*

Patchwork blocks finished separately – 3-D

At one point I got bored with always making the neat little rows of patchwork blocks and the tidy little patchwork sheets and wanted to try something more free. So I finished a block, sealed and quilted it separately as a small piece almost like a pot holder. I finished others and then attached them to each other at the corners, leaving a space between them so that when they were hung on a wall it would also contribute to the composition. Baby Blocks (fig. 221) is an example of this. Baby Blocks is very difficult to sew, with so many angles and no straight seams. You have constantly to pick up the needle of your sewing machine and turn it, and tease the corners in. So I finished off each block separately, quilted it

and attached it to the others at the corners. I made long strips for the borders. It is interesting to see how the quilt changes if it is placed in front of a dark wall or a light one.

Figure 222 shows another experiment using this technique. I took the traditional Flying Geese pattern, shown in figure 39, and made two separate strips in red, white and blue using this motif. The background is made of red and blue stripes with white frames, and the whole design and its movement come from the attachment of the two separate bands. The free form gives it a much more intense feeling of motion.

My favourite experiment was to make

221 *3-D Baby Blocks (above left)*
222 *3-D Flying Geese (above right)*

Flying Geese as a mobile (fig. 223). I wanted to give the impression of free-flying birds. I made six chains of triangles in various shades of purple and red, and they turn freely in the wind. The eye actually fills in the small triangles which are missing, and the pattern is very much alive and changing.

Paint on patchwork
Another technique is to take a plain-coloured material and paint on the patchwork pattern. With an eye for detail

223 *3-D Mobile Flying Geese*

you can easily duplicate the design using a variety of paint techniques, and the paint lends an interesting feeling of superficiality to the patchwork design.

Miniature quilts
I have seen some very interesting work by a Spanish textile student who tried to make miniature quilts no more than 20 cm by 30 cm in size. She took all the detail of the full-sized quilts and made them in miniature. It was charming to see them and they made beautiful wall decorations. It is difficult to work with the small pieces, but that is part of the challenge. Miniature tapestry has become very popular over the last ten years, and miniature patchwork is also worth working with.

Sculptured quilts
Quilting can be used in much the same way as tapestry. One could make a very large mural design by piecing together four or five large finished panels. Indeed, I had to make a large piece for the lobby of a hotel in Jordan measuring $3\frac{1}{2} \times 5\frac{1}{2}$ metres. It was not technically possible to make such a large piece, so I made a sampler quilt with six

224 *Spring Weave (above left)*
225 *Church Window (above right)*
226 *3-D Stars and Stripes (opposite)*

different designs all using the same colours, burgundy, beige and brown, and attaching the six pieces only as it was hung.

I could imagine making a walk-in quilt where you arrange pieces around a centre structure. Circular- or triangular-shaped quilts would be another way of modernizing design.

3 Incorporating ideas from other art forms

It is often possible to take ideas from other art forms and make them your own by translating them into patchwork. Homage to Vasarely and Homage to Joseph Albers (figs 25 and 215) are two examples where the inspiration came from a painter's work, the first from op art, and the second from the colourist school. The idea for Porto (fig. 67) came from the tiles painted on the sides of houses in Porto, Portugal.

Spring Weave (fig. 224) shows an idea taken from weaving. The background is plain, cream-coloured fabric with an olive-green frame in the middle of the quilt. The pattern comes from eight strips which have an olive-green stripe and light olive printed flowers. After quilting I wove them in and out of each other and then fastened them into place exactly where the green frame came in to give it a border.

Wooden doors
Purity (fig. 115) was an idea taken from a wooden door. Woodwork is constructed from many separate elements and is therefore ideal as a subject-matter for patchwork.

Stained glass windows
Church stained glass windows are constructed by using different small pieces of coloured glass and is also a good subject-

Schapper

matter. One lady I met in Holland makes small renditions of stained glass windows in patchwork, complete with black frame to emphasize the colour and design (see fig. 225).

Flags

Since flags were originally made of patchwork you could also look to flags for inspiration. Each country, state, city and very often even local clubs have their own flag. You could copy them directly, or reduce them in size and repeat the same flag changing the colours, or you could make the whole collection of world flags as a type of living encyclopaedia. Figure 226 shows my version of the American flag. The base quilt is red and white stripes with a navy-blue border, and the stars are made separately in navy-blue material and attached to each other and hang freely, turning in front of the striped background.

Games

Another interesting idea is to make games within the quilt design. You could make all kinds of board games, like snakes and ladders, or card games, like bridge. The design could be purely decorative or it could be functional. Figure 227 is a small patchwork version of checkers and pachisi made in India.

4 Combining other mediums and techniques

Another possibility is to use other techniques in combination with patchwork and quilting.

Embroidery, with its combination of colourful threads and decorative stitches, can add a lot to the potential beauty of a quilt. Examples of this are Crazy quilt (fig. 206) and Fan quilt (fig. 213) and the sample of appliqué from Sri Lanka (fig. 33).

Smocking, tucking and folding

One of my ambitions is to make a quilt using smocking, which looks so pretty on young girls' dresses. One block could be made of smocking, another with regular

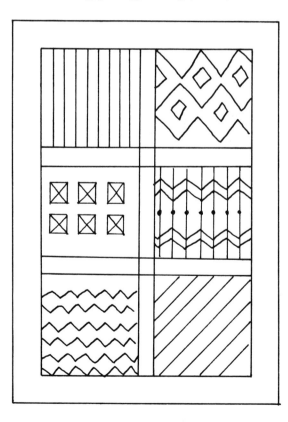

227 *Games (above)*
228 *Smocking, folding, tucking (below)*

tucks, embroidered, and another with tucks and decorative stitches (fig. 228). This would make a charming patchwork quilt for a very feminine bedroom.

Woven pieces
In Sri Lanka one of the more commercially popular ideas is to quilt locally woven material. It is fresh looking, in strong colours, and usually has a pattern of irregular stripes. The strong pattern and texture, together with the filled quilt, make an appealing combination of techniques.

Crochet or knitting
Blocks for patchwork could be made easily on a knitting machine in either cotton or wool. There are so many beautiful Jacquard patterns and other possibilities.

Crocheted blankets are very often made up of squares, so this makes it ideally suited to quilt design. Quilting either knitting or crochet work can be interesting and attractive.

Batik
Batik is a fabric-printing process using wax which results in charming, bold designs and colours and offers many possibilities for quilts.

Silk-screen printing
Silk-screen printing as the basis for patchwork quilts has been used successfully in America. One artist recently made a silk-screen print of Marilyn Monroe on a white material in the manner of Andy Warhol's famous image, and then quilted it.

Photographs would be very popular as a silk-screen image, school class photographs for instance, with each quilt square containing a different photograph. Round the World (fig. 108) would be charming if each block was the same photograph repeated in a different colour.

Silk-screen printing can be done with modern designs, or more traditional ones, if you prefer. Printing your own ideas and quilting them afterwards would give you complete freedom of design.

Braiding
I met a German tapestry artist who had worked in Africa and had become fascinated by the way the women braid their hair. He started to imitate their braiding in tapestry. Although cotton gives you less freedom, it would be interesting to cut cotton fabric into strips and braid them into patchwork blocks. The early Americans made rugs using this technique.

Reducing the quilt vocabulary
Another possibility for experimenting with the design of patchwork is to leave something out of the way the quilt is made.

Using the same fabric Usually when doing patchwork you take different fabrics in different colours to make the pattern. It would be novel to take the same material and cut it up into patches, sewing it together as if there were differences in colour and design. The seams would break up the colour, and different grain directions would result in an intriguing quilt. This would be especially successful with a plain-coloured material, but a patterned one could also be used.

Using one piece of material Another idea, instead of making the pattern out of patchwork, take just one piece of material and quilt the patchwork pattern onto it. If you were going to make Autumn Leaves for example, then outline the design and quilt it into the plain material (see fig. 229).

5 Using current subject matter
Many of the historical quilts to be seen in American museums are charming because they depict some historical event, the end of the Civil War, the election of a president, the making of the Constitution and so on. Our modern quilts would also benefit from some current event being depicted on them.

The daily news is full of events which we could show pictorially in quilts: the Pope's travels, the Common Market leaders getting together, the royal wedding, the birth of Prince William – all these would be valid subjects for a quilt.

Current events also happen in our own lives. A baptism, marriage, golden anniversary all tell a story of something happening now. My first effort at appliqué was to make nine blocks commemorating my parents' thirtieth wedding anniversary. I made one block depicting their meeting day, one for their wedding, one of their house, and one for each of my four brothers and sisters and myself, and the last one of their anniversary.

Figure 230 and colour plate 14 show two sampler quilts. These are more traditional designs, but a sampler could be made to show some event happening at present.

In colonial times many everyday household things were made into quilt designs: a butter churn, logs for the fire, canoes, log cabins, tea or coffee cups. It would also be an idea to update this by making a quilt out of squares with, for example, alarm clocks, televisions, washing machines, cars, aeroplanes, records, radios, boats, helicopters, or even a can of soup, bottles of Coke, etc. We could use motorcycles, roller skates or things we use every day, like detergents, soap or even an iron.

The easiest method is to cut out the shapes and appliqué them to a background but you could try to translate these objects into geometry if you do not want to use appliqué. Anything can be translated into triangles and squares. It may not be recognizable, but the pattern may be worthwhile on another level.

What I have demonstrated in this chapter is that ideas for designs are everywhere. Once you feel comfortable with the technique, and start to have confidence in your imagination, you will find many ideas. You may get tired and think you have run out of ideas but making one quilt usually leads to another. Sometimes you get blocked. Take a rest, read a book, go to a museum, take a train out to the country. The chances are that the title of the book, or an exhibit in the museum, or a particular shaped building you pass will give you a new idea. It may not hit you like lightning, but little by little, and ideas will start growing and you will be on the way to developing your own style.

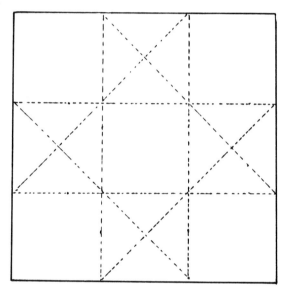

229 *Quilting without patchwork (above)*
230 *Sampler quilt 2 (opposite)*

117

7

My parting advice

I hope I have passed on some of the love and enthusiasm I have for this craft. I stumbled on it by accident, and was lucky to have had two men to help me: Ahmed, a Lebanese quilter who showed me the technique, and Walter, my Swiss husband who helped me to learn design.

I have learned several things over the past seven years' involvement in my craft.

1   Never give up hope. Even though you may feel hopelessly bored or lonely, work a little every day. The mere fact of being able to accomplish something will help you to get out of whatever problems you might have.

2   Everyone is creative. Many of us had strict fathers or husbands or a bad school experience and believe we are not creative. I have seen a child drawing figures on steamed-up car windows, and instead of encouraging any hidden artistic talents, his mother, a good German housekeeper, said, 'Oh Karsten, isn't that wonderful that you are helping me clean the car windows!' Creativity is the same as sensitivity. It is the feeling of authority to take things and put them together in a way we like. My first love is naive painting. When I saw funerals in Beirut, I didn't want to see all the grief and sorrow, so I painted happy, bright-eyed people walking to the cemetery amidst beautiful valleys and flowering trees. I painted it the way I wanted to see it. Textiles also give you the chance to create

one of several different moods. Believe in yourself and keep working!

3   Trust your own taste. You may receive criticism of your work. The criticism may be justified, or it may be made from jealousy, or some other strange reason. Please yourself.

4   Plan well. I have shown you the technical side and how to assemble colours. Nothing beautiful is built accidentally, and the notion that you can just grab any old rags, work five years on it and have a beautiful quilt, is inaccurate.

5   Sign your quilt. I always sign mine even though the old cigar-smoking aunts of the colonial time did not believe in signing theirs. My name means I am proud of it and testifies to the fact that I have done the best job I could.

6   Know that you are part of a big movement. Women everywhere do patchwork and like patchwork, whether it be of a practical nature, repairing clothes or blankets, or of a more artistic nature. It is every bit as valuable to sew a quilt, as for your husband to go to an office building or drive a truck.

7   In closing, remember to respect tradition, but do not be strangled by it. Never mind what traditional design or technique demands. We are living in the twentieth century, and you are an artist in your own right, and don't let anyone tell you differently.

Index